a signed edition from

GREAT  ORTHERN

THE GIN CLAN

SCOTTISH GINS & DISTILLERIES

FIONA LAING

GREAT NORTHERN

Fiona Laing has been writing about food and drink in Scotland for more than a decade. At first, whisky was the drink of choice, mainly as she worked with a Bangalore-based distiller who introduced the first Indian single malt whisky to Europe. The other spirits and wine were never far behind as she travelled the world, listening to the stories of the makers. Travel writer, food editor, hotel judge, Fiona has explored food and drink whenever her career as a newspaper journalist and PR consultant allowed.

Great Northern Books Limited
PO Box 1380, Bradford, BD5 5FB
www.greatnorthernbooks.co.uk

© Fiona Laing 2019

ISBN: 978-1-912101-48-1

Design and layout: David Burrill

CIP Data
A catalogue for this book is available from the British Library

CONTENTS

SCOTTISH GIN

Every week it seems there is a new gin launched into the market. And a good proportion of them are Scottish.

My research shows that in Scotland 23 distilleries went into production in 2018, with at least 12 more due to come on stream in 2019. In addition, there were another 18 new gin brands launched. Overall, 2018 saw 41 Scottish debutants in the marketplace. Add to this the fact that nearly every established brand released at least one new limited edition, and it has made for a lively segment of the Scottish spirits world.

Why is Scotland such a powerhouse of modern gin? I think there are several factors which come into play – history, whisky, expertise and Scotland's natural resources all have their part. There is also an energised community of gin makers who love exploring the rich botanical world and creating enjoyable flavours.

Most importantly there is a market. It is made up of the increasingly knowledgeable gin drinkers who continue to seek out new experiences, alongside a more general thirst for consumable products which reflect the place they come from and a respect for artisan skills. There is also an interest in products that come from Scotland.

WHAT'S SCOTTISH?

What makes a gin Scottish? Is it using heather, thistle or pine needles? Or water from a Highland burn? Is it making the base spirit from scratch? Does the juniper need to be picked in Scotland? Does the distiller need to be Scottish? Does the distillery need to be in Scotland?

These are the elephants in the room – and that herd makes it a pretty uncomfortable place at times.

Unlike whisky, the industry is not tightly tied up in rules and regulations, so there is no legal definition of what constitutes Scottish gin – in fact, there is hardly even an informal consensus about it.

This might be in part from the realisation that if it is defined too tightly – "made with Scottish-made spirit" or "made using Scottish juniper" for instance – there will only be a handful of gins that qualify. So where is the line to be drawn?

Many people and organisations have views and we will look more closely at the debate in another chapter.

In this book, I have neatly sidestepped the dilemma by classifying the entries under the headings "The Clan" and "Kith & Kin".

The Distilling Clan consists of the distilleries – its members have a still in Scotland, and they use it to make gin.

The Kith & Kin are the rest: the gins we think of as Scottish. There are makers, creators and brand owners who have gin made for them in Scotland – and elsewhere. There are cuckoo distillers who make their gin on other people's stills. And there are makers who use compounding techniques to create "bathtub" gins.

The classification is not perfect, but it is a neat reflection of the Scottish gin family in 2019.

WIDE CONNECTIONS

There are certainly plenty of reasons why Scotland should be involved in the modern gin boom. If you look at its history, you find gin has significant roots here.

On the one hand there is the Dutch connection. Just across the North Sea, what is now the Netherlands, was historically one of Scotland's closest trading partners. Jenever, the juniper spirit that is the forerunner of gin, would have arrived aboard the ships docking in ports such as Aberdeen, Dundee and Leith.

Such was the volume of trade that in 1782, records show 2.5 million gallons of jenever being imported into Scotland.

But it wasn't all one way; in the 18th and 19th centuries, juniper grew so profusely across the Highlands that the East Coast ports were sending large quantities of it to the Low Countries for use by the Dutch.

There was also likely to have been a home-grown version of jenever and some of the spirit drunk – particularly that from illicit stills hidden from the Excise men in the hills and glens – would have been a form of flavoured spirit using ingredients found locally.

Scots were often soldiers of fortune and would have fought with – or against – the Dutch and been aware of the jenever-fuelled "Dutch courage" of troops who were said to have drunk their ration before going into battle.

The sea is another reason for gin's connections to Scotland. As the country's industries developed, using raw material from around the world and sending its finished goods abroad, the sea ports flourished. Thirsty sailors required something to drink both at sea and on land.

With indifferent water supplies, spirits and ales were the answer and distilleries congregated in the dock areas where they had easy access to raw materials.

Around Edinburgh's port of Leith there are records of eight licensed distilleries in 1777, but there were probably another 400 illegal stills in the area as well.

Ships would carry spirits for their sailors to drink. On naval ships the gin had to be at Navy strength (57% ABV) so that if the gin spilt and the gunpowder for the cannons got wet, it would still light.

When, in 1867, it became a legal requirement for sailors to have a daily citrus ration, it was in Leith that Rose's Lime Juice was created which went perfectly with the officers' gin ration.

Gin was also a favourite drink for Scots living abroad, especially in malarial areas where quinine – a defence against malaria – was made palatable with gin.

The Scottish diaspora – soldiers, sailors, engineers, traders, civil servants, teachers, missionaries – found a taste for gin with their quinine tonics.

SPIRIT OF ADVENTURE

For many people, the thing they will associate with Scotland's distilleries is whisky. After all, Scotland exported the equivalent of 1.23 billion bottles in 2017 according to HMRC data.

Yet, gin is intrinsically tied to whisky, sharing many of the same processes and technology.

Distillers were key players in the Scottish economy in the 18th and 19th centuries, satisfying both domestic consumption and exporting their spirits. But they were also at the mercy of the wider economic conditions and changes to the tax regime.

At the height of the Gin Craze in the early 18th century, Scots were taking advantage of the thirst for spirits.

Two families – the Steins and the Haigs – were dominant in Scottish distilling and had much of the home market sewn up, so they looked further afield.

In 1777, records show James Stein exported 2,000 gallons of spirit to

Photo: Strathearn Distillery

England to be "rectified into gin". By 1782, the figure was 184,000 gallons and it is said that by 1786 Scottish production accounted for a quarter of the English market.

In 1786, when extra duties were imposed on Scottish spirits, sales in England collapsed and it hit the Steins.

However, the family bounced back, and by 1826 Robert Stein had invented a still capable of a continuous method of distillation. This was the seed for revolution in the industry and meant greater quantities of better quality spirit.

Refined by the Irishman Aeneas Coffey with the introduction of a twin column still, the need for multi-distillation was removed and the quality of the spirit improved again.

Distilleries founded by the Stein-Haig dynasty – John Stein married Margaret Haig in 1751 – are today the sites of modern gin operations. In the north of Fife, Seggie was founded by William Haig in 1810 and is now the site of Eden Mill. Further south, John Haig founded Cameronbridge in 1824: it is now the largest grain distillery in Europe and home to Tanqueray and Gordon's Gin.

Today, three of the world's bestselling gins – Gordon's, Tanqueray and Hendrick's – are all made in Scotland.

Which helps explain the often-quoted statistic that 70 to 80 per cent of the gin produced in the UK comes from Scotland.

THE MODERN BOOM

Gin might have largely gone out of fashion in the 20th century but James Bond and Gordon's kept it in the consciousness.

People started to become more interested in gins again as they found Bombay Sapphire in the 1990s and, when the premium gins such as Hendrick's and Tanqueray No Ten were launched as the new century dawned, there was a renewed appetite for the old favourite.

When legislation changed and allowed smaller stills, the artisan or craft gin makers stepped up. At the end of this century's first decade, it was the whisky makers who were among the first to test the water – Caorunn, the Botanist, Darnley's and Edinburgh Gin came from companies with established whisky brands.

Today the makers are from all walks of life: from farming and hospitality to the military and marketing – there is no pigeonholing a gin maker.

There are some solely focused on gin and there are a number established as whisky distilleries who are making gin while they wait for their whisky to mature.

Reasons to make gin are again as numerous as the entries in this book. The dreams of the makers are what fuels much of Scotland's gin boom.

There are the farmers looking to diversify their livelihood, the entrepreneurs wanting to celebrate their beautiful hometown and the gin enthusiasts who wanted to have a go themselves.

Most interesting are the people who have founded distilleries to enhance their community – to invest sustainably in future generations, protecting a way of life and creating employment. Isle of Harris and GlenWyvis spring to mind, but there are others.

Island life can be fragile, and the inspiration for Isle of Harris Distillery in Tarbet has been to create a thriving enterprise to strengthen the economy and community.

GlenWyvis, a community-owned distillery, hopes to help regenerate Dingwall and plans a visitor centre to attract the tourists enjoying the North Coast 500 route.

And then there are the gins created to raise money for good causes. From

disadvantaged young adults or military charities to environmental concerns to medical research, again the reasons and the amounts raised vary.

Of course, for some, making gin is the purely commercial addition of a brand to a portfolio of drinks.

Whatever the reasons, it all adds up to the overall picture of gin selling like the proverbial hot cakes.

Wine & Spirits Trade Association figures show that sales in the UK in the 12 months to November were valued at £1.93 billion. The summer heatwave of 2018 can only have helped push the total to 66.3 million bottles – up 41 per cent on the same period the previous year.

Industry experts are just waiting for UK sales to break the £2 billion barrier.

An interesting trend which the WSTA figures highlight is the growth in the popularity of pink and flavoured gin. The data shows that flavoured gin has driven over half the growth in gin, despite only making up one-fifth of total sales. And almost three-quarters of flavoured gin's contribution to that growth has been driven by pink gin.

Some say the next trend will be savoury flavours. At least in Scotland, the gin scene already caters for the widest range of tastes.

Photo: Deeside Distillery

UNIQUE INGREDIENTS

Scotland's modern gin boom owes much to whisky. Distilling is a big industry but in the second half of the 20th century it was dominated by established distilleries and large international players.

In terms of employment options, any dream of becoming head distiller at a Speyside or Islay distillery would be hard to achieve, while going it alone and setting up your own distillery was out of most people's reach.

Regulations on minimum still size dating back to the Gin Act of 1751 meant entrants to the market needed to set up a large operation backed by deep pockets and substantial funds.

Then in London, the founders of Sipsmith, inspired by the craft spirit makers of the United States, took on HMRC in order to be granted a licence to produce gin in small quantities. The distillery opened in 2009 … and the craft spirits revolution began in the UK. The smaller stills changed the business model and we've seen several distilleries created in Scotland – and there are more in the pipeline.

With the tight rules around making Scottish malt whisky – it must be distilled twice in a copper pot still from barley, yeast and water and matured in oak for at least three years – it means a long-term investment before you see any return. This is where gin comes in. It can be made in a matter of days and be bringing in cash soon after.

Strathearn, Glasgow, Eden Mill and Isle of Harris, are just some of the whisky distilleries which have launched gins while waiting for their malt to mature. And there are more to come: in Edinburgh alone, Holyrood, Port of Leith and Crabbie's have distilleries being built and gins already on the market.

Scotland's established whisky tradition has given us significant expertise in distilling which has been another key factor in the growth of gin here. Some of the expertise is passed down in person and gained from hands-on experience, but Scotland also has one of the world's most respected centres of academic expertise.

ACADEMIC EXCELLENCE

Heriot-Watt University has crafted an enviable reputation for its International Centre for Brewing and Distilling (ICBD). The centre which traces its roots back to 1904, when courses in brewing were first offered, operates as a strong partnership between industry and academics. It is the only organisation in the UK to offer Honours and Masters degrees in distilling and brewing. Students take advantage of a well-equipped pilot distillery and a full range of analytical equipment and labs as they study. There are also plenty of industry projects undertaken.

Not surprising then that numbers have been increasing in recent years with a record cohort of 104 MSc students on campus in 2018-19. In the five years to 2018, 387 students graduated with an MSc and the interest of those graduates has increasingly been focussed on gin. Dr Annie Hill, associate professor at the ICBD, notes that she only had one student gin project in 2012 but by 2018 there were 13.

Working with industry comes mainly in two forms – student projects and formal consultancy, with Dr Hill and her colleague Matthew Pauly widely quoted by industry figures for their invaluable contributions.

The UK's Knowledge Transfer Partnership (KTP) programme helps businesses improve their competitiveness and productivity through the better use of knowledge, technology and skills. Many businesses form KTPs with universities.

Edinburgh Gin formed a KTP with the ICBD when it set up its distillery in the capital. Head distiller David Wilkinson was the KTP associate from Heriot-Watt and oversaw the process of taking a gin concept through recipe design to full scale commercial production.

Another of Heriot-Watt's headline partnerships was where Kirsty Black went on to make her MSc project into Arbikie's first gin – once she had set up the distillery, where she is now head distiller.

Strathearn Distillery's founder Tony Reeman-Clark turned to Heriot-Watt for advice while setting up his distillery in Perthshire. "They were a tremendous centre of experience, learning and help," he says.

The university was also at the heart of the formation of what is now the Scottish Distillers Association (SDA), of which Mr Reeman-Clark was the first chairman. It grew out of the links being forged between the academics and the new distillers setting up their distilleries.

A common interest group was formed with the support of Interface, the organisation which connects business with Scotland's academic world. Some of the group's activity was a purely practical sharing of knowledge – getting through red tape or working out wiring – alongside understanding the science and being able to talk about flavour profiles confidently.

The Scottish Craft Distillers Association (now the SDA) was the formalised result but the legacy is wider than that. Scotland's gin community has a collaborative and supportive feel and several makers talked to me about experiencing – and benefitting – from this informal network. One distiller who had worked with other craft drink makers said it was a welcome surprise to encounter so much support when he started on his gin journey.

BOTANICALS

An important piece of Heriot-Watt research which SDA members can call on is the Scottish Botanical Library. In a project set up with the help of Interface, it is a reference database of more than 70 seeds, roots, fungi, berries, fruits and herbs that can be grown sustainably in Scotland. It has detailed notes on taste, aroma and mouthfeel for each entry which was individually distilled.

"We have a knowledge of how plants behave when they are distilled and what sort of attributes they bring to a gin," explains Dr Hill. "It will make product development much faster. If people want to produce a gin that has particular attributes, we know which plants they can use to get that profile."

The library also has data on non-native core botanicals, such as juniper and coriander, from a range of different sources. The number of Scottish botanicals included will be increased and further work is being added on toxicity. Dr Hill is quick to point out that botanicals are at such a low concentration in a gin you would have to drink so much of it that you would be dead from alcohol poisoning before you get anywhere near the danger levels of a particular ingredient.

She says: "It's a way of advising companies on which botanicals to choose. It will depend on the export market: if you're planning on sending it to the United States, then you avoid botanicals that are not on the Food & Drugs Administration's approved additives list."

NATURAL RESOURCES

Scotland's botanicals are only part of the natural bounty of the country. There is clear pure water, filtered through ancient rocks or from the sky and unpolluted streams. Just as it was important to the early whisky distillers, this is often quoted by gin makers as one of the unique characteristics of their spirit.

But it is the botanicals which are most often giving the makers something to talk about. Scotland has so many different types of habitat and each has its own set of unique botanicals. From the shoreline itself, through the sandy dunes and rich lowland pastures, grain, fruit and vegetable crops, to the grazed uplands, the Highland heather moors and forests – every few miles you travel there is something different for the gin maker to forage.

And juniper – the basis of all gin – grows in Scotland but there is far less of it than there once was. Makers who know of wild bushes are being careful not to be specific on location – for one thing, they need the berries for their future gins – but also wild native juniper is under threat.

The Forestry Commission for Scotland says that juniper has been struggling because many plants are over a century old and so produce fewer seeds. On top of that any young plants are a target for deer, sheep and rabbits. As juniper needs male and female bushes to pollinate, sparse growth reduces the chance of new bushes. There is also a deadly disease, *Phytophthora austrocedrae* which is spreading.

Several gin makers are planting juniper so that there is a Scottish crop to harvest and use but it takes several years to become established.

On Skye, when Sir Iain Noble pioneered the establishment of one of Scotland's first native woodland regeneration schemes, he made sure native juniper was included in the planting. For Pràban na Linne, the distillery he founded, the juniper's progress towards maturity is being closely monitored.

Botanicals allow gins to reflect the place they come from, an attribute that has been likened to the terroir of French wines. This chimes well with Brand Scotland's place in the food and drink industry where provenance and high quality are its selling points.

While many Scottish gins have botanical links to their home, others call on the rich history and romance of their birthplace. Names have their roots in their area's myths and legends with strong branding developed

Photo: Glaswegin

around that story. You'll come across many examples as you read about the gins in this book: it's a broad sweep though Scottish folklore.

BRAND STORIES

Getting that branding right in the increasingly crowded market is an important step on the road to success. And it is good to see that gin owners can use Scottish resources for graphic design, bottle decoration and packaging.

Some labels are the work of a talented individual artist, while others are from industry-leading design agencies. One such design agency is Pocket Rocket Creative in Stirling where Del Sneddon, Gary Dawson and Gary Doherty have worked with some of the biggest names in drinks since they set up in May 2007. Such is their creativity and innovation, you would never believe it is the same team working for each of their high-profile clients.

Others turn to designers outside the industry for a fresh perspective. One of the most impressive of recent launches is the striking Glaswegin bottle designed by Paul Gray of Suisse Studio, in Glasgow. He is probably best known for developing an emergency shelter to house people in warzones or natural disasters and his work on museum exhibition space.

Another creative resource often used by Scottish gin makers is the Crieff-based Glass decoration specialist, Image on Glass. Under the direction of founder John Henderson, it now produces 1.5 million hand-decorated bottles – both glass and ceramic – a year, having been founded in 1997. Its roll-call includes at least 25 gin brands.

Once the brand is complete, there are plenty of opportunities to get it out in front of consumers. Tasting events, festivals, cocktails, gin bars and specialist bottle shops all give us the chance to enjoy Scotland's gins.

TOAST TO THE FUTURE

There really is no doubt that Scotland is riding the crest of a gin wave. But what does the future hold?

Like gin's past, its future will be determined by a host of external influences over which we have little control.

For Scottish gin, there are both challenges and opportunities ahead. And many makers are set on a course that will take full advantage of the opportunities in exploring botanicals, brand expansion and developing gin tourism. In the wings, there are new makers set on joining the industry, bringing with them their own ideas.

However buoyant things are, there is also a realisation that ultimately the boom is unlikely to go on for ever. There is a need to make sure things are set up in the best way possible to protect the sector from whatever the future holds.

As I researched for this book, I asked people what they saw as the challenges ahead and the responses were mostly around "provenance" and "regulation".

Of course, there are other issues such as saturation of the market, changing tastes and whether flavours are being taken too far.

Then, there is the whole question of discretionary spending on non-essential purchases. It can't go unnoticed that the interest in gin has grown at the same time as confidence in the UK economy returned after the financial crisis of 2008. How long will the good times continue?

Never has the United Kingdom had greater uncertainty about our place in the world. Discussing Brexit and Scottish independence has changed our international outlook and it doesn't take a crystal ball to know they will have an influence on the future.

PROVENANCE

In recent years, consumer priorities have been shifting; more people are interested in the details of the products they buy: where it comes from, what is in it, how it is made, who makes it.

The focus is provenance. As you will see in this book, Scottish gin really chimes with those interests – the stories about the makers and their gin journeys reveal the details of the "where", "what", "how" and "who".

What the people in the industry are worried about is the transparency around that provenance and clear labelling of what is in the bottle. There should be no question of where a gin named after a place comes from. What's inside should be there on the bottle in black and white.

So, Scottish gin should be made in Scotland...

But what about picking all the botanicals in Scotland and then making the gin in England? Does that count? What about a gin named after a croft where all the botanicals are picked but it is made 200 miles away in a city distillery?

Very quickly you see where the muddy waters develop.

This matters because Scotland has a reputation. Scottish whisky is a global leader and many of our other products are seen as the best in the world. Whether it is salmon or Arbroath smokies, haggis or Aberdeen-Angus steaks, soft fruits or shortbread, Irn-Bru or Tunnock's Caramel Wafers, Scotland implies top-quality food and drink.

What most industry figures have said to me is that it is the transparency around the provenance – whatever that is – which is vital.

Alan Wolstenholme, chair of the Scottish Distillers Association (SDA) and honorary professor at the ICBD, said: "I go along with the definition that to be called Scottish, something should be made in Scotland."

He adds: "I believe in transparency and the customer should be getting what he believes he's getting and if he's getting something with a Scottish name or place name, I don't think it should be made in another country."

Some people go further. They feel that if a gin is not made in the place it says on the bottle, that is taking advantage of the good reputation of Scottish gin and extreme cases deserve to be called out.

REGULATION

So do we need regulation around Scottish gin? To consider that you have to go back to the very definition of gin.

The European Union defines "distilled gin" as one made by redistilling alcohol of agricultural origin with an initial strength of 96% ABV in stills traditionally used for gin in the presence of juniper berries and other natural botanicals. The juniper taste must be predominant. London gin and London Dry gin are types of distilled gin with nothing added after distillation apart from water.

Photo: Verdant Spirit Co

Alongside that is "gin", a juniper-flavoured spirit drink produced by flavouring neutral alcohol of agricultural origin with juniper berries and other natural substances. Again the taste must predominantly be that of juniper. This includes what is referred to as "compound" or "bathtub" gin.

In the EU, the minimum bottled strength for "gin" and "distilled gin" is 37.5% ABV. This book concentrates on those gins. There are also "juniper-flavoured spirit drinks" – including Dutch jenever or genever – with their own rules and bottled at a minimum of 30% ABV.

What is causing debate is the stipulation for a "juniper-led" flavour.

As people become more and more adventurous in their choice of botanicals, the juniper flavour can almost disappear, and, as many point out, if you leave out the juniper it is just a flavoured vodka.

Hayman's Gin hosted a debate to discuss the place of juniper in gin in September 2018, having launched a campaign to "Call Time on Fake Gin".

The concerns aired raise the possibility of establishing a tasting panel to evaluate juniper content. That, of course, brings up a host of further issues. In the meantime there is self-regulation and consumer education.

Compared to Scotch whisky with more than a century of regulation, gin has very light rules and plenty of scope for innovative interpretation. And many people are loath to dampen that spirit of creativity. The debate will continue.

Another area of concern is that you see the word "gin" used on products that are obviously not gin. There have even been non-alcoholic brands launched which make a play of being "not gin". And liqueurs can often make much of the gin part of their brand, although they contain very little gin.

All this might not matter to the consumer if they enjoy what they are drinking, but other makers are concerned about the potential damage to the reputation of their premium product.

This does lead on to discussions around the need for a legal definition of Scottish gin. There are several options which might be available.

A Geographical Indication (GI) show that products have a specific geographical origin and possess qualities or a reputation that are due to that origin. They are internationally recognised.

In Scotland, at the beginning of 2019, there were 14 GIs including Arbroath smokies, Scotch beef, Scotch lamb, Shetland lamb, Stornoway black pudding and Scotch whisky.

"I think we would struggle to establish GI status for Scottish gin as, unless you say there is something particularly different about it, it wouldn't qualify," says Alan Wolstenholme of the SDA.

An accreditation scheme – which would tell consumers that the gin in the bottle was distilled in Scotland to certain criteria and in a reliable manner – is more practical.

This is where the SDA is working to introduce a code of practice and associated accreditation mark across the spectrum of Scottish distilling.

"The accreditation will help consumers have confidence in the quality and craftsmanship which has gone into the spirit they are choosing," adds Prof Wolstenholme.

In the meantime, people still get hung up on the detail of what makes a gin Scottish.

Scottish juniper? Scottish-made spirit? Scottish-grown botanicals? Scottish distillery? Gins meeting all those criteria would mean we had a very slim book and even the people who could meet that standard agree Scottish gin would not be any better for too narrow a definition.

There are people who have tried to classify gin into categories of Scottishness. The independent not-for-profit Scottish Gin Society has an excellent website listing gins under five classifications which were particularly useful when I started out on this book.

The society differentiates between gins distilled in their own distillery in Scotland and those contract distilled here and outside Scotland. It also lists those that are "cuckoo" distilled at someone else's distillery and compound gins.

James Sutherland, owner of Edinburgh gin bar 56 North and one of the figures often called on for his experience and knowledge of Scottish gin, has looked more deeply at provenance.

He highlights the "grain-to-glass" distilleries where they do everything themselves from making their own base spirit and redistilling with botanicals. Some may even grown their own ingredients for a "field-to-glass" gin.

Next he sees "Scottish distilled" gin made by Scottish distillers with a Scottish still but, as they buy in the GNS and may use non-Scottish botanicals, there may be very little in the bottle grown in Scotland. This is what most gins tend to be. He also points to the use of Scottish botanicals and place names in gins made elsewhere. Like others in the industry, he particularly wants to see transparency around this.

In my own research I've noted that some gin makers are on a gin journey: they have a dream but are taking small steps towards it. Investing in distilling equipment, setting up a space to use it in and obtaining the required licences requires an investment of both time and money.

Having a gin recipe made first by an established distiller before building their own distillery is a route you'll come across. Among the Kith & Kin there are eight gin makers with distilleries under construction and at least four of the Clan have only moved production to their own stills in 2019.

The bottom line is that it is transparency which is important. Alongside not being sure how much of a brand's gin is made at its own distillery – rather than contract made elsewhere – one of the most frustrating things for me has been the distillers who will not confirm whether "island botanicals" are actually picked on the island or are just ones that can grow there.

Luckily, the majority of Scottish gin makers are happy to explain – in great detail – the lengths they go to pick their hero ingredients.

So, is there some existing means by which the naming of Scottish gins could be regulated? Advertising, trading standards or food standards rules could perhaps be used. Whether there is a desire to take action is the question.

The issues around provenance and regulation are pretty certain to get the gin community animated when they gather, but most of the time their minds are fixed on how to distil their next taste-tickling batch of gin. And there are plenty of opportunities for them.

OPPORTUNITIES GALORE

Scotland's wealth of botanicals will always inspire gin makers – the quest for new flavours to entertain the drinkers is easy to satisfy when you have so many different habitats growing wonderful plants. There is no doubt more gins will be made in Scotland.

There also seems to be a belief that there is space for more sales, but that for established brands the opportunity is not in adding new flavours but in exploring new markets. For some that is looking at wider distribution,

SPICED
- ssia
- .beb
- ove
- .min
- ack tea leaf
- riander
- nger

CITRUS
- mon peel
- weet orange

BERRIES
- derberry
- owan berry
- loe berry

HERBAL
- juniper
- rosemary
- thyme
- sage
- oregano
- nettle

FRUIT
- sea buckthо
- mulberry

ROOTS
- orris root
- angelica root
- milk thistl

FLORAL
- rosehip
- lavender
- marigold
- lemon balm

Photo: Darnley's Distillery Gin School

for others securing supermarket space and for others it will mean exporting.

The word of caution here is that the interest in provenance is not limited to Scotland, so consumers in other places will be attracted to their own local gins. This means Scottish gin needs to be of the highest quality to compete.

As sales become more remote, how a gin is presented is almost as important as the way it tastes. Not everyone will have had the opportunity to smell, sip or talk about the product before they buy the bottle, so it has to have shelf appeal.

As we all know, a touch of tartan sells. I shamelessly wanted it on the cover of this book as it's a familiar shorthand for Scotland, but there is a wealth of other material to call on.

Scotland has a strong historical narrative, beguiling folklore, distinctive clothes, accents, customs and whisky. Films like *Braveheart*, *Rob Roy* and *Mary Queen of Scots*, TV series like *Outlander* and books like *The Da Vinci Code* put Scotland in the international spotlight. Our sporting life – golf, tennis, rugby, football – takes the brand across the world. All this means the door for Scottish gin is ajar. To push that door, needs strong branding, as well as that transparent provenance and high-quality gin.

GIN EXPERIENCES

Alison Higgins of the Scottish Gin Society, among others, points to the opportunities for makers in developing gin experiences.

"Someone who comes through your door, experiences the workings of your distillery and your gin first hand means you have a brand ambassador walking out of the door," she says.

Again the whisky industry has lessons for gin makers. The Malt Whisky Trail on Speyside was devised in the 1950s and has successfully enticed visitors to explore whisky – not just in the North-east but ultimately throughout Scotland. In 2017, whisky tourism was said by the Scotch Whisky Association to be worth £60.9 million with 1.9 million visits to Scotch Whisky distilleries.

And gin has picked up many tips. Many makers welcome visitors to their distilleries and share their secrets – some will even let you make your own gin.

There are now gin distilleries right across the country with visitors bringing a much valued boost to their community. For example, Isle of Harris Distillery had more than 91,000 visitors in 2018 – as an island location, this shows the potential.

Edinburgh will be the test of that potential as it sees five new distillery visitor centres prepare to open from 2019. Holyrood, Port of Leith, Crabbie's, Edinburgh Gin and the Johnnie Walker Experience have all drawn up plans which include visitor facilities. Of course, these are not solely appealing to the gin audience but targeting whisky tourism as well.

Outside the capital, the variety of locations for gin experiences means a very pleasant itinerary for anyone wanting to explore Scotland.

CELEBRATING SCOTTISH SUCCESS

One of the nice things about the Scottish gin scene is the busy calendar of events.

Scotland's first gin festivals were in 2014 when the Juniper Festival launched in Edinburgh, and the folk behind the Stirling Whisky Festival replicated their successful format for gin. Since then, there has been a steady stream of events.

In 2018, among the first-timer we saw the Whisky Lounge introduce a Gin Lounge concept; the Edinburgh Corn Exchange launch its own Big Big Gin Festival and True OriGINs put the spotlight on gins made in Scotland.

In 2019, the Gin Cooperative is making sure International Scottish Gin Day will take the Scottish gin message to an even wider audience. On 3 August, distilleries, bars, bottle shops and drinkers are invited to celebrate Scottish gin – in any way they choose.

As the interest in gin has increased so has the number of awards. I could write a whole book about awards that Scottish gins have won but I haven't. In fact, I've largely ignored them.

That's because there are so many of them and I'd be sure to have just missed some when we go to print. The gin makers themselves lose no time in shouting about any they win, so I'll leave it to them.

All that said, awards do matter and in my eyes the ones that concentrate on Scottish gins seem most relevant here. The Scottish Gin Awards were launched in 2017 by KD Media and quickly won a place in our hearts.

Scottish Gin Awards 2018

Distillery of the year: Isle of Harris Distillers

Gin of the year: Eden Mill Original Gin

Gold medal gins: Original Gin, Eden Mill; Misty Isle Gin, Isle of Skye Distillers; Still River Uncut, Deeside Distillery; Boë Scottish Bramble Gin Liqueur; Makar Cask Aged Gin Matured in Mulberry Wood; McQueen Mocha Gin

Best Newcomer: Beinn an Tuirc Distillers

Scottish Gin Awards 2017

Distillery of the year: Arbikie Distillery

Gin of the year: Verdant Dry Gin

Gold medal gins: Verdant Dry Gin; El:Gin; NB Gin Navy Strength; Makar Cask Aged Gin, Matured in Oak; Makar Old Tom; Rhubarb & Ginger Liqueur, Edinburgh Gin

www.scottishginawards.co.uk

Photo: Gerardo Jaconelli

THE
DISTILLING CLAN

Clan (a tribe or collection of families subject to a single chieftain, commonly bearing the same surname and supposed to have a common ancestor)

These are the gin distillers of Scotland. They have a physical still on Scottish land where they make gin. They may also make other spirits – so there are several whisky distilleries, as well as makers of rum, absinthe, vodka and liqueurs. In some cases, they make gin for other brand owners under contract, or they may allow "cuckoo" distillers to use their stills to make gin. In one case the distillery only makes gin for other people.

The distilleries are listed by their name or company's name – not necessarily the name of the gin.

56 NORTH

[56 North Distillers Editions, South Loch]

Edinburgh
fiftysixnorth.co.uk
First gin: January 2018
Tours available

As gin bars go, 56 North has one of the most impressive collections – 400 bottles and counting.

It is a result of being in business for more than a decade and James Sutherland's enthusiasm for all things juniper.

In 2018, the venue that had served up so many glasses of gin, went a step further and added a distillery to its bar.

The two copper pot stills have initially been used to produce seasonal Distillers Editions in 100-bottle batches – and perfect the recipe for the signature gin.

South Loch, a classic London Dry-style gin with a twist, was launched in the spring of 2019.

Under the guidance of distiller Lindsay Blair, a Heriot-Watt graduate, the Distillers Editions will continue alongside the new gin, meaning guests will always have exclusive new gins to explore.

34 · THE GIN CLAN

APOTHECARY
[EiDYN]

Quartermile, Edinburgh
www.apothecary-bar.com
First gin: June 2018

The science behind making gin is not that far removed from the early days of medicine when the apothecary would concoct potions and tinctures from herbs and minerals.

In Edinburgh, what was once the site of the Royal Infirmary is now a complex of office, residential and leisure spaces and home to a bar called Apothecary. It comes complete with upstairs distillery and brewery.

Part of EiDYN, a chain of city bars and lodgings, Apothecary's gins include lemongrass and heather editions alongside a classic juniper-heavy named the Author.

There is also a range which includes rum, vodka and non-alcoholic distilled botanical drinks.

ARBIKIE DISTILLERY

[Kirsty's Gin, AK's Gin]

Inverkeilor, Angus
www.arbikie.com
First gin: July 2015

When you are a commercial potato grower what do you with your wonky veg? Make gin was the answer for the Stirling family at Arbikie.

As the Stirlings supply the major supermarkets, potatoes that didn't match the specified criteria would be rejected – meaning that up to 25 per cent of the crop would be wasted.

Farmer Alec Stirling's sons John, Iain and David are the driving force of the distillery project. However, it is also a testament to their master distiller Kirsty Black.

After a decade working in the medical devices industry, Kirsty was studying for her brewing and distilling degree at Heriot-Watt when she was introduced to the Stirlings.

She did her Masters project with them, designing what is now Kirsty's Gin, and then project managed the conversion of a farm building into the distillery.

The distillery is unusual in that it is a single site operation – the ingredients for all its spirits are planted, sown, grown and harvested within an arm's length of the building and the water is taken from an underground lagoon on the estate.

They are making gin, vodka and whisky from their harvest and all the spirits are distilled in the same copper pot stills, with the vodka and gin spirit going on to a 40-plate distillation column.

Kirsty's Gin is notable for using potatoes in its base spirit, giving it a smooth creaminess – and there are 6kg of spuds in a bottle.

Its key botanicals reflect the ocean, rock and land of the area. The kelp comes from the seashore, Carline thistle from the rocky coastal soils and blaeberries are found around the farm.

AK's Gin was devised around Alec's favourite flavours – honey and ginger and its spirit is made from wheat grown on the farm.

The fresh honey comes from nearby hives and black pepper and smoked cardamom substitute for the ginger.

In everything they do, the Stirlings embrace a field-to-bottle process and work is underway so that they will be able to welcome visitors to the distillery to show what that means in practice.

BADACHRO DISTILLERY

[Badachro Gin]

Gairloch, Wester Ross
badachrodistillery.com
First gin: January 2017

As love stories go, the Badachro one deserves to have given birth to a delightful gin. It was in the remote Highland hamlet on the shores of the Gairloch that Gordon Quinn met his wife Vanessa many moons ago and it is where, after years of globetrotting, they now live.

Their gin marries botanicals handpicked from the surrounding hills, woodland, fields and shores of the Gairloch with pure Highland water in a "rather mature" copper pot still called Delilah.

Their gin journey started when they had settled in Badachro in 2006 and were running a holiday business.

They were thinking about souvenirs for guests and as Gordon says: "We started to hatch a plan to make a scent from local botanicals … that idea morphed into a gin."

Munich-born Vanessa calls on her work in horticulture and study of botanicals while Gordon employs the expertise he gained at a Perthshire distillery learning about the craft.

Together they have used wild myrtle, coriander, gorse blossom, lavender, rose-hip petals, elderflower and juniper to help create their distinctive gin and capture the "purity, clarity and wonder of their stunningly beautiful land".

The original hand-crafted gin with its marriage of floral and herbaceous notes has been joined by Badachro Gin 57° Storm Strength which is a match for any cocktail.

BADVO DISTILLERY
[Badvo Gin]

Pitlochry, Perthshire
www.badvo.com
First gin: July 2018

Badvo Gin is not the first spirit distilled on the hill farm outside Pitlochry. Family records detail how previous generations had flavoured spirits with whatever grew around them.

However, it was a welcome endorsement for Helen Stewart's decision to set up a modern distillery on the land her family has worked since 1599.

And more important in that decision was the fact that the farm is a rich source of botanicals – including juniper – and has a supply of clear spring water.

It would also be a valuable diversification for the family business.

Like many teenagers, Helen had gone off to university to study – English – and worked to control her student debt – in a distillery.

Already making good use of the resources to hand, her dissertation was on the "linguistic legacy illicit distillation left in whisky and gin".

Returning home, Helen set about her plan – gathering business advice, grants, experimenting with botanicals, transforming an outbuilding, installing a still and hiring her first employee – her mother.

Not bad going before the age of 24 and, in fact, Scotland Food & Drink and NFU Mutual gave her the Inspirational Young Person Award in 2018 for her talent and dedication.

For Badvo Gin, Helen forages all of the botanicals herself, using nettles, rowanberries, apples, meadowsweet, honeysuckle and wild mint to create a herbaceous gin with a mint finish.

The purity of the farm's spring water was the inspiration for Badvo's logo. Only pure spring water can support enough fish for a heron.

BALMENACH DISTILLERY

[Caorunn]

Cromdale, Morayshire
www.caorunngin.com
First gin: August 2009
Tours available

A rare type of still is an important part of making gin at one of Scotland's oldest legal whisky distilleries.

The 1920s copper berry chamber was designed to extract essential oils to use as a base for perfumes.

The spirit vapours pass through its four botanical trays at a very slow rate which ensures the maximum uptake of the flavours and aromas of the botanicals.

When one of Balmenach's distillers Simon Buley starting thinking about making a gin, he first considered the idea of making it in the working whisky distillery.

Instead, a separate gin plant was established where Simon – now the Caorunn gin master – could harness the uniquely pure water and the traditional Celtic botanicals from the hills nearby.

With Simon picking those botanicals himself, it meant that when Caorunn was launched it was one of the first of the hand-foraged Scottish gins.

And one of those botanicals – rowanberry – was to give the gin its Gaelic name.

Using the one-of-a-kind still to make Caorunn in small batches allows the rowanberries, heather, Coul blush apples, dandelion and bog myrtle to work their magic with six traditional botanicals.

The Celtic botanicals give a contemporary edge to the full-bodied London Dry-style gin.

BARDOWIE DISTILLERY

[Bardowie Gin]

Bardowie, Stirlingshire
www.hazellandhazell.com
First gin: December 2016

When the home you live in was once the site of an illicit still, it is almost inevitable that you consider the idea of making gin. Especially if, like Mark and Alison Hazell, you are already in the drinks industry.

The Hazells' home sits beside Bardowie Loch to the north of Glasgow.

In 1822, the *Glasgow Herald* reported that Excise men discovered "a complete set of utensils necessary for distillation" at the lochside and apprehended two smugglers who were taken to Stirling and "lodged in jail".

Mark is a man of the country and the Hazells' table is filled with whatever is in season, so when they started to think about making gin, they looked to the land around their home.

Experimentation led to Bardowie Gin which uses blackcurrant, bay, bullrush stem and ground elder from their doorstep, together with juniper berries, coriander, angelica root and orange.

Until 2019, the Hazells had been making their London Dry-style gin at other distilleries including Strathearn. Now that they have their own still, they can develop other gins and put their sustainable ideals into practice.

As the owners of the Jaw Brew in Glasgow, a microbrewery which is run on the circular economy model, they can extend those principles to the distillery.

For example, Mark and Alison will use the wash from the beer making – rather than neutral grain spirit – in their gin.

However, life has already turned full circle as their outhouse is now home to a legal still and distillation has returned to the loch – almost 200 years since the Excise men's raid.

BEINN AN TUIRC DISTILLERY

[Kintyre Gin]

Torrisdale, Kintyre
www.kintyregin.com
First gin: June 2017
Tours available

Looking across Kilbrannan Sound to Arran from the Torrisdale Estate, you know you are somewhere special.

From the hill to the shore, the land on the Kintyre peninsula has been in the ownership of the Macalister Hall family since 1872.

A series of diversification projects has allowed it to continue as an unspoilt part of Scotland's West Coast.

The Beinn an Tuirc Distillery is the latest in that line of innovations and it operates sustainably to protect its environment.

Named after the highest point on Kintyre, it is housed in a former piggery and powered by the estate's hydro-electric scheme.

Under the guidance of head distiller, Su Black, batches of Kintyre Gin and its expressions are distilled on Big Don, the 230-litre copper pot still imported from Germany.

Each batch is named, rather than numbered: the first after place names significant to Kintyre. The second used local slang words and dialect, which have been used to create an entertaining series of films on YouTube.

Kintyre Gin has ten traditional botanicals plus two which grow in abundance on the estate.

Sheep sorrel provides sweetness and pleasant floral aromas, while Icelandic moss – actually a lichen – adds green notes to the London Dry gin.

Expressions include one aged for three months in a first-fill bourbon barrel from Heaven Hills, the Kentucky whiskey company. This Oak Aged Kintyre Gin has subtle caramel and vanilla notes.

Adding Scottish oats and raspberries in the distillation creates the Kintyre Pink Gin, with its hints of the summer dessert cranachan.

BENROMACH DISTILLERY

[Red Door Gin]

Forres, Moray
reddoorgin.com
First gin: July 2018
Tours available

Speyside is the beating heart of Scottish whisky, with 50 of the world's best known distilleries lining the banks of the Spey and its tributaries.

One of the smallest working distilleries is Benromach. With its distinctive red doors, it dates back to 1898 although it had been mothballed in 1983.

It was purchased in 1993 by the Urquhart family which owns Gordon & MacPhail the Elgin-based bottler, wholesaler and retailer.

Since then the distillery has built an international reputation for its classic Speyside malts.

Now the distillery's red doors have an additional spirit behind them – Red Door Gin. The London Dry-style gin is distilled on Peggy, a baby version of Benromach's copper whisky pot stills.

The distinctive small-batch gin, which has a citrus bite from bitter orange and lemon peel, uses juniper, coriander, angelica, sea buckthorn, heather and rowanberries.

BLACKFORD CRAFT DISTILLERY

Rothienorman, Aberdeenshire
www.blackfordcraftdistillery.co.uk
First gin: October 2017

[Vesperis Pictish Gin]

You can't visit the north-east of Scotland without encountering the legacy of the Picts, whether it is one of their intricately carved stones, a hill fort, a place name or a legend from their Dark Age Scotland.

Blackford Craft Distillery sits in the Picts' heartlands, inspired by their tradition of brewing and mead-making.

Developed by Neil and Katie Sime, the distillery is home to an iStill called Genevieve which is making vodka and gin but also has the capacity to ferment and so opens up the possibility of making cider.

The still room is in a redeveloped steading and there are plans to renovate the rest of the space into a warehouse and office and create a tasting room.

First off the still was a vodka made using a flavour profile derived from Picts' heather mead. It is distilled with organic heather honey, wild harvested heather and seasonal organic apples.

This was followed by Vesperis Pictish Gin, made with the same apples, honey and heather along with botanicals including juniper, coriander seeds and lemon peel.

As the Picts were astronomers, who observed the planets to track the seasons, the Simes looked to the heavens for inspiration for their brand name.

Vesper was the personification of the Evening Star – or Venus – in the mythology of the Romans, who as it happens never managed to conquer the Picts.

BOË GIN
[Boë Scottish Gin & Boë Violet Gin]

Stirling
boegin.com
First gin: 2007

First there was Boë Superior Gin – launched way before the explosion in craft gins by VC2 Brands. Named after Franz de la Boë, the 17th-century Dutch physician credited with the invention of gin, the brand did well – being served at some of Scotlands's top hotels and bars.

However, until 2015, it was not the top priority for VC2, which also owns Black Wolf Brewery. It was then that Boë's sales started to rise as the interest in craft gins grew. Seeing its potential, Carlo Valente, one of the founders of VC2, started to experiment with flavours, knowing that only an exciting new concept would do.

Carlo came up with a violet coloured gin, smelling of sweet violets, with a distinct taste of juniper and a lingering finish of lavender and ripe berries.

At its launch in 2017 there were no other flavoured or coloured gins, so it certainly had the wow factor Carlo had been looking for.

In 2017, VC2 installed a gin still next to its brewery and it now makes all of its gins, including its flavoured gin liqueurs.

Boë Scottish Gin has taken the place of the original Superior gin, but it keeps a similar style and flavour profile.

Alongside juniper, there's coriander, angelica, ginger cassia bark liquorice and star anise, orange and lemon peel in the triple-filtered gin.

THE BORDERS DISTILLERY

[William Kerr's Borders Gin]

Hawick, Roxburghshire
www.thebordersdistillery.com
First gin: August 2018
Tours available

For 180 years legal whisky distilling had been absent from the Scottish Borders. In March 2018, the situation changed when the Three Stills Company commissioned its whisky distillery in Hawick.

Located in the town centre, a £10 million restoration of the former Hawick Electric Company has created a fully functioning distillery and visitor centre.

Like many new whisky distilleries, the company's first release is a gin.

William Kerr's Borders Gin is made using the distillery's own malted barley-based spirit in a specially commissioned Carter Head still with a copper basket that suspends the botanicals.

It celebrates a Hawick-born botanist who is one of Scotland's most respected 19th-century plant hunters.

In those days Scotland had a reputation for producing fine botanists, nurserymen and gardeners and Kerr, like many Scots before him, was recruited by the Royal Botanic Gardens at Kew in London.

In 1804, he went to Asia where his work earned him his reputation. He sent back 238 plants new to European gardeners and to science.

The gin named in his honour combines 11 botanicals including juniper, wetlands myrtle, citrus peel, cassia bark, coriander seeds, angelica, heracleum sphondylium (hogweed or cow parsnip) and liquorice root.

BRUICHLADDICH DISTILLERY

[The Botanist]

Isle of Islay
www.bruichladdich.com/the-botanist
First gin: January 2011

As Islay distilleries go, Bruichladdich has one of the most stunning settings, right on the shore, looking out over Loch Indaal.

In a community steeped in whisky tradition, its outlook however is deliberately progressive.

The birth of the Botanist is a good illustration of this intention to shatter expectations. It was Islay's first gin – and one of the first from a Scottish whisky distillery.

The distillery itself dates back to 1881 and in 1994 was shut down.

With the new millennium, came owners with a vision to transform the semi-derelict site into a modern operation which went on to set the whisky world alight.

Creating the Botanist was a complicated process. Head distiller Jim McEwan experimented for more than five years before settling on the balance of nine core and 22 Islay botanicals, wheat-based neutral grain spirit and water from Dirty Dottie's spring on Octomore Farm.

The technicalities of distilling this complex recipe also called for innovation.

When people talk about a bespoke still rarely do they mean something like Ugly Betty.

Brought from a grain distillery in Dumbarton, the 15,500-litre Lomond still had originally been designed as a flexible tool.

However, it still took serious modifications to create something that would satisfy Jim's gin vision and exacting standards.

Ugly Betty's 17-hour distillation creates a complex gin where the botanicals – including chamomile, creeping thistle, bog myrtle, downy birch, elderflower, gorse, hawthorn and heather – each have their place.

CRABBIE & COMPANY

[Crabbie's Gin]

Leith, Edinburgh
crabbiewhisky.com
First gin: December 2018

Crabbie's is probably now most famous for its ginger wine and beer but once the man behind the name was one of Scotland's most important whisky makers. And like many distillers of the 19th century, John Crabbie also made gin.

The brand, now owned by Halewood Wines & Spirits which includes Whitley Neill gin in its portfolio, has returned to its roots in Leith where it once had extensive bonded warehouses and a whisky blending business.

Already operating from the Chain Pier Distillery in nearby Granton, a new distillery is set to open in the summer of 2019, with its own single malt whisky due to join Crabbie's existing range of bottlings of other distilleries' malts. Neatly, the site itself has strong whisky credentials as it was once a distillery owned by John Haig.

The gin now being made under the direction of Marc Watson, the distillation and maturation manager, is based on a recipe in John Crabbie's own handwriting from the company archive. Marc, a Heriot-Watt graduate who brings experience from Eden Mill and Shetland Reel, says that finding the recipes was too good an opportunity to miss. "We think gin and flavour has come so far but, in fact, these recipes prove we haven't strayed too far at all."

He adds that they tinkered with the recipes for the London Dry-style and Old Tom gins "to make them more balanced and moreish".

Using a 600-litre Holstein still, both have eight traditional botanicals with something much more unusual – sea salt from the Isle of Skye. The result is that Crabbie's signature gin has a light citrus tang, a hint of dry spice and a smooth finish.

The Old Tom has more coriander, angelica and orange peel added after distillation before being aged in a sherry butt.

CRAFTY DISTILLERY

[Hills & Harbour Gin]

Newton Stewart, Galloway
craftydistillery.com
First gin: June 2017
Tours available

From the rugged tree-clad hills to the rocky sand-fringed coast the south-west corner of Scotland is often seen as a hidden gem. Galloway is certainly a gin maker's treasure house. This fact was not lost on Graham Taylor when he looked at the feasibility of setting up a distillery in his home town.

The rich store of botanicals and ideal tourist destination meant he felt he could do something unique and do it with integrity. The new purpose-built distillery and stylish visitor centre makes the best of the views and reflects the eye for detail of Graham who has a background in branding and design. That detail starts with Crafty making its own spirit onsite from wheat supplied by a Galloway-based farmer.

The two hero botanicals in Hills & Harbour Gin are harvested close by. The bladderwrack seaweed is collected about 25 miles away and the noble fir needles seven miles away.

Created by distiller Craig Rankin, Hills & Harbour was the result of at least 90 test recipes and 14 months of experimentation. There are a total of 11 botanicals including dried mango, which acts as a natural sweetener, and green Sichuan pepper and bay leaf to excite the senses.

Because they make their own spirit, the gin takes about 13 days to go from grain to glass.

The glass around the gin is a bottle which cleverly seems to capture both the green of the forests and turquoise of the sea.

Product developments saw a classy Galloway Gin limited edition at the end of 2018 and an innovative non-gin product was due in early 2019.

CROSSBILL'S HATCHERY

[Crossbill Gins]

The Barras, Glasgow
www.crossbillgin.com
First gin: November 2014
Tours available

The story of Crossbill spans more than 140 miles. Now based in the urban heart of Glasgow, its roots are in the Highlands.

Jonathan Engles was captivated by the tradition of harvesting and distilling juniper from the Scottish hills.

In the 18th century it had been harvested for export across the North Sea to the Dutch distillers who produced jenever.

Native juniper is now a rare find in Scotland and Jonathan was one of the pioneers of distilling it when he first made Crossbill Gin on the Inshriach estate near Aviemore.

In 2017, he moved into his purpose-built distillery and gin school in the Barras.

He is now expanding the original unit and adding a second still, bar and a botanical greenhouse which will be heated with the waste heat from the distilling process.

Crossbill Gin might now be made in the city but it still uses Highland juniper alongside rosehips for a London Dry-style small batch gin.

Named after the finch which lives in the Scots pine forests of the Highlands, Crossbill has been joined by several special editions.

For one, Jonathan infused Crossbill with staghorn sumac, a botanical he foraged in New Hampshire, to create a gin celebrating the habitat of the North America red crossbill – a cousin of the Scottish crossbill, whose adult males are a distinctive brick-red and females greenish-brown.

DALTON DISTILLERY

[Oro and Oro V gin]

Dalton, Dumfriesshire
www.orogin.co.uk
First gin: May 2018
Tours available

The gold at the end of the rainbow is something many of us hope to find. For Ray Clynick, however, his golden goal was the best gin he could make.

With a Masters degree in chemical biology, Ray set about his quest in the most scientific way possible.

Also a Heriot-Watt distilling graduate, Ray used his knowledge of flavour compounds and his understanding of the distilling process to devise and test recipes.

After distilling many variations and conducting extensive consumer tastings, he was left with two gins of equal quality.

One he called Oro, which translates into gold in both Italian and Spanish, the other Oro V.

These gins are made at his family-owned distillery where the scientific approach is evident.

For instance, the purpose-built pot still is fully coppered because copper is proven to ensure the flavour compounds are separated out and delicate notes not lost.

There is also a Lab where the experiments for future releases take place.

Science is even in the company branding: the logo uses concentric circles to represent the atomic suborbital structure of gold itself.

Nothing is left to chance while the gin is created with 100 per cent British grain spirit, macerated for 24 hours and slowly distilled for more than 15 hours.

Oro has 15 botanicals – juniper, vanilla, coriander, cinnamon and pink peppercorns among them – and its taste was designed to change depending on the volume of tonic added.

Oro V is a more modern style of Dry gin, with lavender acting as a smoothing agent making it ideal for sipping neat.

Dalton Distillery, however, is not all science: the food and drink served in the tasting rooms, bar and terrace are much more intuitive and receive great reviews.

DARNLEY'S DISTILLERY

[Darnley's Gin]

Kingsbarns, Fife
darnleysgin.com
First gin: 2010
Tours available

For Darnley's, it is about connections. A Fife family – the Wemyss – with a castle overlooking the Firth of Forth and colourful ancestors, had a drinks portfolio into which gin would fit.

Calling on the expertise of Charles Maxwell of the Thames Distillery and drinks writer Geraldine Coates, William Wemyss had Darnley's View created.

The gin called on the family's heritage, in particular Wemyss Castle where it is said Mary Queen of Scots had her first encounter with the man who was to become her husband, Lord Darnley.

Using botanicals – including wild elderflower – found around the castle, a light, fresh floral, citrus London Dry gin was produced.

By 2017, with the family's whisky distillery newly established in a farm on the Cambo estate at Kingsbarns, there was the opportunity to bring Darnley's View home to Scotland.

Since 2017, Darnley's – as the gin has been rebranded – has been distilled and bottled in the separate gin distillery.

Darnley's gin distiller Scott Gowans has faithfully recreated the Thames recipe on the new Frilli still housed in a renovated cottage which also hosts the Darnley's Gin School.

Scott, who is a product of Heriot-Watt and has worked at breweries as well as gin distilleries, launched Darnley's first Fife-created gin in the

summer of 2018. The Very Berry edition of the Cottage series uses botanicals from around the Kingsbarns site.

There is a hint of the sea – from the sugar kelp which is farmed off the nearby coastline – among the fruity notes delivered by sloe berry, rosehip and elderberry.

The Cottage series sits alongside Darnley's Spiced Gin which takes its inspiration from further afield with ten botanicals from as far afield as Africa and China.

It honours the Wemyss family's spirit of adventure and naval service including that of Sir Rosslyn Wemyss who became First Sea Lord in 1917 and Admiral of the Fleet in 1919. This gin – with more juniper added – is also bottled at Navy strength.

DEERNESS DISTILLERY

[Sea Glass Gin]

Newhall, Orkney
www.deernessdistillery.com
First gin: May 2017
Tours available

At first it was demijohns and brewing kits, now Stuart and Adelle Brown have a full-blown distillery, taking their long-standing hobby to a new level.

Everything at Deerness Distillery is personal – it was designed by Stuart, an Australian chartered engineer, and built by him and Adelle, a pharmacist, and their family, friends and neighbours.

The gin (and vodka) being made there is entirely created, distilled, bottled and labelled by the couple, who moved to Orkney in 2014.

The gin is cut with purified Orcadian water which is produced by a reverse osmosis system, designed and built by Stuart.

Inspired by the landscape around them, Sea Glass Gin has seven botanicals and the Browns intend to grow five of them – cucumber, mint, lavender, lemon leaf verbena and tarragon – in their own polytunnel.

The name reflects the time they enjoy with their young children collecting "sea glass" on the beach.

The handmade Portuguese copper stills – Walt, Zing and Matilda – are beside the visitor centre, which, alongside their own drinks and distillery merchandise, also stocks Orcadian and island-crafted gifts.

In their operations, the Browns are as sustainable as possible, for instance using recycled packaging and supporting small businesses in their community.

They are also supporting Scapa100 which commemorates the 100th anniversary of the scuttling of the German High Seas Fleet in Scapa Flow off Orkney.

Scuttled Gin uses juniper, tarragon, cassia bark, lemon peel, chamomile flower heads, green pepper, lavender and mint in London Dry-style gin bottled at 43% ABV.

A percentage of the profits from Scuttled will go to Scapa100 so that future generations can be educated about the event.

DEESIDE DISTILLERY

[Still River gins]

Banchory, Aberdeenshire
www.facebook.com/stillrivergin
First gin: August 2017

Few of Scotland's gin makers make their own grain neutral spirit so the fact that the Deeside Distillery does sets it apart.

It was craft ale that opened the door to this option for Michael Bain who in 2012 founded the Deeside Brewery, which quickly attracted a loyal following for its small batch ales and lagers.

The distillery was launched in 2017 and uses a by-product of the brewing process to make its own grain neutral spirit.

With this the distillery creates its range of Still River gins, including Naked, Uncut, Rhubarb, Spiced Plum and a special edition Dee Gin.

The flexibility of the distillery set-up means the gins, which were previously marketed under the Twin River name, have rums and fruit liqueurs – and ultimately whisky – as siblings.

Under the guidance of head distiller Liam Pennycook, Deeside has been making headlines in the gin world.

Uncut was the world's strongest gin – at 77% ABV – when it was launched in 2018.

Then a keg cocktail for the distillery's own Sessions festival turned out to be a record sized G&T of 875 litres.

DELIQUESCENT

[ChiQuiOui Gin]

Kelso, Roxburghshire
www.deliquescent.co.uk
First gin: October 2017

Scotland's first micropub – officially defined as a one-room public house – also has a microdistillery.

Rutherford's is the bar in the Borders market town which has been serving cask ales and unusual drinks in traditional but quirky surroundings since 2015.

Owners Simon and Debbie Rutherford distil in a handmade 200-litre Portuguese copper still, although they do admit their gin-making method of choice is bathtub style.

They feel compounding the gin gives them more flexibility over flavour and fun for their small batches.

Their signature ChiQuiOui gin is smooth and juniper led, with the zest of grapefruit and oranges and delivers a cheeky bit of their sense of fun.

Other full strength gins include a colour-changing Rose Gin, a shimmering Parma violet expression and a haggis gin launched for Burns' Night 2019.

However, it was a Merry Berry Gin – berry flavours mixed with Christmas spices – which kicked it all off.

DIAGEO

[Gordon's, Tanqueray, Jinzu]

Cameronbridge, Fife
www.diageo.com
First gin: 1998

There's no doubt that Diageo is the biggest gin maker in Scotland. Quite how big is hard to unravel as Cameronbridge is said to be the largest grain distillery in Europe, but alongside Gordon's and Tanqueray it also makes spirit for its whisky brands.

The distillery was originally founded by John Haig in 1824 and thanks to adopting the innovative Coffey column stills, was a key part of the Haig whisky empire which ultimately became part of modern-day Diageo.

It was in 1998 that Diageo consolidated much of its UK white spirit operations – notably Gordon's, Tanqueray and Smirnoff vodka – to Cameronbridge and its nearby bottling plant in Leven.

In 2019, Gordon's celebrates the 250th anniversary of Alexander Gordon founding his distillery in the Southwark district of London.

Alexander was one of the first makers to place the emphasis on the quality of the natural botanicals, leading a seachange in the image of gin.

With its high juniper content, Gordon's was for much of the 20th century, the gin everyone drank. Its classic crisp clean taste works well with tonic and it is said that, somewhere in the world, a bottle is sold every six seconds.

Although it was created in 1830 in London, all Tanqueray gin is now made at Cameronbridge. The original recipe that Charles Tanqueray developed in Bloomsbury is unchanged but it is now crafted by master distiller Terry Fisher and his team.

Its four botanicals – juniper, coriander, angelica and liquorice – are at the heart of each of the expressions which have been launched in recent years.

Tanqueray No Ten is made on a small copper pot still known as Tiny Ten using chamomile and fresh orange, grapefruit and lime for a citrus burst.

In Leven, where there is an experimental distillation lab, Jinzu, Diageo's gin-sake hybrid spirit, is made.

It was invented in 2013 by Dee Davies, the winner of Diageo's bartenders' competition.

It blends a gin featuring juniper, coriander, angelica, yuzu and Japanese cherry blossom, with sake for a creamy mouth feel and a subtle sweetness.

DISTILLUTIONS MICRO DISTILLERY

Arbroath, Angus
www.distillutions.com
First gin: January 2018

Distillutions is unique in that it doesn't make its own gin. The micro distillery turns other people's dreams into gin.

It could be for a luxury hotel, a shop or a bride looking for unusual wedding favours and Lewis Scothern will craft the perfect gin.

A graduate of Heriot-Watt's brewing and distilling course, Lewis has worked for some of Scotland's leading craft breweries and distilleries.

The opportunity to set up his own distillery in his home town – and in Angus with its world-wide reputation for high quality food and drink – was too good to miss.

With a 50-litre still for development, Distillutions can scale up recipes for distilling on its 200-litre modular still.

There is also a bonded warehouse for the storage of spirits in duty suspension.

In his first year, Lewis collaborated with several Angus companies and saw the gins they created together nominated for – and win – awards.

So far, he has no plans for launching his own gins as he enjoys the satisfaction gained from collaborating with his clients on their own projects.

DORNOCH DISTILLERY

[Thompson Brothers Organic Highland Gin]

Dornoch, Sutherland
www.thompsonbrosdistillers.com
First gin: November 2017

Crowdfunding has played an important part in the life of the Thompson brothers, Simon and Philip.

Not once, but twice, it has helped them on their distilling journey. They set up their whisky distillery with the help of a money-raising round in 2016.

It was a dream come true for the malt enthusiasts who run a highly regarded whisky bar at the Dornoch Castle Hotel.

Between fulfilling crowdfunders' whisky orders and transforming an old fire station into a distillery, the pair undertook extensive research with their backers and created a gin.

After a series of Experimental batches, they launched Thompson Brothers Organic Highland Gin which is made using spirit distilled in-house from heritage barley.

It is a blend of 90 per cent organic grain spirit and 10 per cent organic floor-malted heritage barley, slowly fermented and twice distilled on copper pot stills.

The grain spirit is combined with the brothers' special botanical blend and slowly distilled.

The new make spirit is then combined with the base gin spirit and slowly diluted to 45.7% ABV.

The botanicals include juniper berries, angelica root, cardamom seeds, aniseed, orange peel, lime peel, lemon peel, coriander seeds, meadowsweet, elderflower, black peppercorns and freeze-dried raspberry.

The gin is presented in a bottle based on a 19th-century fire grenade.

That nod to the distillery's origins may soon be out of date as the brothers launched a second crowdfunding initiative in 2018.

It will allow them to move to a larger site close by and create a better production area, as well as space for tours, shop and tasting room.

DUNNET BAY DISTILLERS

[Rock Rose]

Thurso, Caithness
www.dunnetbaydistillers.co.uk
First gin: August 2014
Tours available

Dunnet Bay Distillery is the birthplace of a gin firmly rooted in its home. Rock Rose was created by Martin and Claire Murray and is based on the botanicals that grow around them in the far north of Scotland.

The gin's inspiration – Rhodiola rosea – is hand-foraged from the exposed cliffs.

Centuries ago, the Vikings harvested it as they believed it would give them the extra strength to continue on their adventures. Today the Murrays use its root, adding a delicate floral note to the gin.

Another plant that is a distinctive feature of Scotland's coastal fringe is sea buckthorn, the silver-leafed shrub that has bright orange berry-like fruit which are prized for their high vitamin C content.

All over Scotland, the brilliant red fruit of the mountain ash or rowan marks the onset of autumn.

Again it has legendary powers: protection against witchcraft and a rowan branch saving Thor, the Norse god after whom the town of Thurso was named.

For Rock Rose, it delicately adds to the gin's berry flavours.

The botanicals are carefully picked and prepared before Elizabeth, the bespoke traditional copper pot still, slowly works her magic.

Following the success of Rock Rose, Dunnet Bay has added seasonal specials as well as Navy strength and sloe gins.

For instance, Lassies Toast is a limited edition to celebrate Burns Night inspired by the moorland tea that Robert Burns is reputed to have enjoyed.

The tea recipe includes bilberry leaves, strawberry leaves, heather tops, speedwell and wild thyme and all of those feature in the Lassies Toast gin.

The distillery has also collaborated and created gins for other people, including the Torridon Estate, the Carnegie Club at Skibo Castle and Partridges of London. It also makes Holy Grass vodka.

In 2017, the distillery expanded its production and bottling facilities and added a gift shop and visitor centre.

EDEN MILL

[Eden Mill Original, Oak, Love and Hop gins]

Guardbridge, Fife
www.edenmill.com
First gin: October 2014
Tours available

Entertaining an American brewer in St Andrews, Eden Mill co-founder Paul Miller realised that the area had no distillery or brewery to show his guest.

When Paul heard that a former papermill less than five miles from the town was available, he'd found the location to plug that gap.

That the mill was originally built as a distillery by William Haig, a member of one of the 19th century's main whisky families, was a bonus.

Opening as a brewery in 2012, Eden Mill started making gin and whisky in 2014. It makes its spirit by hand in copper pot stills, but the gins have been far from traditional.

The first was Hop Gin, introducing the expertise of brewing by using Australian Galaxy hop for a zesty citrus 46% ABV gin.

The original Eden Gin puts seabuckthorn berries found beside the dunes nearby at the heart of the London Dry-style gin.

Meanwhile the contemporary Love Gin is a light blush colour with hibiscus, rose petals and exotic fruits among its hero botanicals.

Oak Gin takes its lead from the whisky aging on site and uses finely cut American oak chips to mature it for up to a week.

In the procession of special editions from Eden Mill, the focus has been on sport – golf, rugby, football – and seasonal flavours.

While the distillery is undergoing a major redevelopment, the emphasis of its visitor experience has been through its Blendworks gin schools in St Andrews and Glasgow.

EDINBURGH GIN DISTILLERY

[Edinburgh, Seaside, Cannonball]

Edinburgh
www.edinburghgin.com
First gin: 2010
Tours available

Edinburgh Gin has not one but two distilleries in the capital – and another at the planning stage.

Beneath the pavements of one of the busiest parts of the capital Edinburgh Gin has been made since 2014.

Below the Rutland Hotel at the west end of Princes Street, Flora and Caledonia – the custom-built copper alembic and column stills – concentrate on making the brand's seasonal products.

During the day, it is where visitors can experience the gin-making process before it becomes a cool cocktail bar as night falls.

In Leith, the former Crawford's biscuit factory has been home to Gin Jeanie, another custom-made copper still, since 2016. With a 1,000-litre capacity, it is where the signature gin is produced.

Edinburgh Gin is a blend of 14 botanicals with lavender, pine buds, mulberries and cobnut giving its trademark twist to its classic London Dry-style.

Unusual botanicals have been a key feature in the development of Edinburgh's expressions.

The distillery was the first to form a partnership with Heriot-Watt University and has called widely on its expertise.

Seaside Gin was created as the result of the collaboration with students foraging shoreline botanicals.

Its scurvy grass, ground ivy and bladderwrack add distinctive minerality to the gin's profile.

Head distiller David Wilkinson called on Heriot-Watt studies when he decided to use frankincense and myrrh to create Christmas Gin.

The spirit of research continues with the 1670 expression a collaboration with the Royal Botanic Garden Edinburgh.

Inspired by the garden's origins as a 17th-century physic garden – a source of plants for medicinal remedies – the gin uses botanicals, including piper leaf, Tasmanian lanceolata leaf and mountain pepper, picked in the modern garden.

The planned distillery and visitor centre will be just off the Royal Mile and is expected to increase distilling capacity by more than 200 per cent.

This is a major investment by Ian Macleod Distillers who bought Edinburgh Gin from founders Alex and Jane Nicol in 2016.

EL:GIN

[El:gin]

Elgin, Moray
elgin-gin.co.uk
First gin: May 2016

El:gin could come from nowhere but the royal burgh which straddles the River Lossie.

The distillery which makes it was founded by a pair of whisky distilling veterans Leah Miller and Paul Hooper who embarked on a journey to make "no ordinary gin".

The result is thanks to Scottish oats helped along by raspberries, strawberries and apples among its nine botanicals.

The fruit and oats come from within a 25-mile radius of their distillery.

The gin has been compared to cranachan, the traditional Scottish raspberry, cream and oat dessert.

El:gin was a deliberate move away from what they saw as traditional "ginny" gins to one that would appeal to the non-gin drinker.

It is distilled in an 80-litre copper pot still over direct heat in a manual process which extends to the filling, sealing and labelling of the distinctive bottles.

The purpose-built distillery draws water from a spring on the rural estate outside Elgin where it sits.

Taking the El:gin lead in using ingredients from close at hand, a range of gin liqueurs and oat vodka have joined the portfolio.

ELECTRIC SPIRIT CO

[Achroous]

Leith, Edinburgh
electricspirit.co
First gin: April 2015

The Electric Spirits Co was always destined to light up the spirits world. James Porteous already knew how to make an impact when he embarked on his brewing and distilling MSc at Heriot-Watt.

He had already had a career in London as a designer after his degree in product design at Glasgow School of Art.

His own gins are packed with style – from creative recipes to the striking bottles. And he offers his design and development skills to bars, restaurants, distilleries and anyone wanting to collaborate on their own bespoke spirit.

Not surprising then that James picked up the Excellence in Branding title at the 2018 Scottish Gin Awards.

In the Tower Street Stillhouse he uses a Genio 500-litre still to make his signature gin Achroous. It is an artisan operation with James at the heart of the hands-on process.

His recipe for Achroous is concise and makes a point of having no citrus

ingredients. The Sichuan peppercorns and fennel seeds add distinctive notes to the five traditional botanicals: juniper, coriander seed, liquorice, angelica and orris roots.

With his creative eye, James has designed the Achroous bottle to stand out behind any bar. The neon orange makes its own electric statement.

Expect to see the Electric Spirit Co starting to live up to its name as James extends his portfolio beyond gin to include vodka, akvavit and absinthe.

ESKER SPIRITS

[Esker Gin]

Kincardine O'Neil, Aberdeenshire
eskerspirits.com
First gin: June 2016

Silver birch sap is the key botanical for Esker Gin. It has also unlocked the distillery's home.

When Steven and Lynne Duthie set up their distillery in 2015, it was in a shed at the bottom of their garden.

Their gin – made with the sap of the trees which are such a feature of Royal Deeside – quickly became a hit.

The need for sap led them to the Kincardine Estate where they gained permission to tap the estate's trees. So, when they were looking for premises to expand, it was the estate which offered them the site of today's distillery.

Using sap as a botanical was a bold move but combined with other botanicals including juniper, pink peppercorn, cassia, rosehip, citrus and heather, it gives the crisp clean Esker Gin a real depth of flavour.

The distillery, which has two traditional copper pot stills, takes a sustainable approach to all it does.

Steve and Lynne operate a zero waste policy, with packaging reused and the waste from the stills given to the estate farmers for use on their fields.

Customers are also offered the opportunity to return empty bottles at events in return for a discount on another purchase.

The bottle itself conveys a sense of the gin's home with the mountains, river, topography, and castles represented alongside those key botanicals.

GLASGOW DISTILLERY
[Makar Gin]

Hillington, Glasgow
glasgowdistillery.com
First gin: October 2014
Tours available

Seven is a powerful number in the world of the Glasgow Distillery. It's the number of times its gin is distilled through its copper pot still; it's the number of botanicals selected for distillation alongside juniper and there are seven sides to its distinctive bottle.

Makar Gin was the first spirit marketed by the company which was set up to revive single-malt whisky distilling in Glasgow, a city which was once a major centre of the industry.

Founded by Liam Hughes, Ian McDougall and Mike Hayward, the distillery released its first single malt whisky in 2018.

It is home to three copper stills – Annie, Mhairi and Tara – each named after members of the founders' families.

Investment was secured in 2018 to allow the distillery to double production with further stills and infrasructure.

The original London Dry-style gin in the Makar range has been followed by cask-matured releases making use of techniques used in the whisky industry to add complexity to the bold juniper-led original.

Continuing the distillery's spirit of innovation, an Old Tom and a cherry gin have joined the line up and a bespoke handcrafted gin called Aquine has been created for Lidl.

Makar means poet in old Scots and, like any piece of verse, each component of the gins and their distillation is the product of careful consideration and attention to detail.

GLEANN MÓR SPIRITS

[Firkin, Glasgow and Leith gins]

Leith, Edinburgh
firkingin.co.uk
theglasgowgin.com
leithgin.com
First gin: April 2014

Gins with personality are the hallmark of the family firm Gleann Mór, which also has a reputation as an independent whisky bottler.

Firkin Gin was the one which kicked it all off. Gleann Mór owners Derek and Karin Mair had always experimented with flavours and when they aged some gin in a firkin, a small-sized whisky barrel, they realised they had something special.

They developed their own signature gin – one which is quadruple distilled using ten botanicals – to work with.

Made at the company's Leith Still House, the gin is rested in oak whisky casks for several weeks, giving it a light golden colour and notes of toffee caramel, vanilla and sweet oak.

Like the whisky industry's trend of experimenting with different finishes, Firkin has gone on to be aged in a range of casks – and is also available Naked without any hint of wood.

It was followed by Glasgow Gin – a modern light fresh and fruity gin which comes in a cheeky bottle featuring "that" image of the Duke of Wellington's statue outside the Gallery of Modern Art - the one with the traffic cone on its head.

The gin, which has 10 botanicals, is made at Langley Distillery in the Midlands but bottled at the Gleann Mór HQ.

Leith Gin meanwhile reflects the port heritage of its home. It's behind the bar at Teuchters Landing, the former ferry waiting room, where Derek and Karin were discussing the need for a straightforward, quaffable gin with friends when the idea was born.

Made at the Leith Still Room, the citrus gin features spicy notes inspired by the far-flung ports of call of the ships which berth at Leith.

GLENWYVIS DISTILLERY
[GoodWill Gin]

Dingwall, Ross-shire
glenwyvis.com
First gin: June 2018

Community is the driving spirit of GlenWyvis: from the first concept, through its funding, to its sustainable approach, the greater good of the area and its people have been at its heart.

Initiated by the "flying farmer" John McKenzie in 2015, the distillery has been established as a community benefit society.

It is 100 per cent community owned with more than £3.2 million invested by 3,200 people, a share of profits will be invested in community projects and it aims to play a key role in rejuvenating the Dingwall area.

Making both whisky and gin, the newly-built distillery uses barley sourced locally and water from an on-site bore hole. Its power is from renewable energy.

When it opened in 2017, the distillery was rekindling the town's tradition of whisky distilling for the first time in more than 90 years. Under the guidance of master distiller, Duncan Tait, production of single malt whisky started in February 2018.

The new building also meant GlenWyvis's existing gins could be made on site in its 400-litre still named Heather.

Launched in 2018, the distillery's signature GoodWill Gin is made with nine botanicals including hawthorn berries picked on a neighbouring farm. The result is smooth and full bodied with a distinct citrus burst.

A limited edition celebrates the North Coast 500 driving route which passes through Dingwall. North Coast 500 is a "more punchy serving", bottled at 50% ABV in homage to the 500-mile drive.

HIGHLAND LIQUOR CO

[Loopallu, Experimental Series, Seven Crofts]

Ullapool, Ross-Shire
www.highlandliquorcompany.com
First gin: September 2018

On the shores of Loch Broom, Scotland's festival scene comes to a close at the end of September with Loopallu, a two-day music-led extravaganza.

In 2018, it also marked the culmination of a five-year dream for Helen Chalmers and Robert Hicks as they launched the Highland Liquor Co.

Loopallu, the first gin from Little Ella, their small copper alembic still, sold out in 24 hours as festival-goers took it to their hearts.

Next up was the Experimental Series, which saw Robert, Helen and their distiller Ben Thompson, a Heriot-Watt graduate, tear up the rule book in a series of one-off expressions.

With a focus on the small West Coast community where they work, the batches take inspiration from the landscape and the people around them.

There is no hurrying. The botanicals are given the time they need to release their optimal aromas and flavours, whether they be from the forests or the orchard or further afield.

And once the spirit has been collected, they wait for it to become rounded before bottling.

With a handful of expressions, the Experimental Series has been paving the way for Seven Crofts to be launched in 2019.

HOUSE OF ELRICK
DISTILLERY

Newmachar, Aberdeenshire
houseofelrick.co.uk
Launched: November 2016

[House of Elrick Gin]

Enquiring minds are inextricably linked to the House of Elrick. Constructed in 1720 at the height of the Scottish Enlightenment, the mansion hosted many philosophical, scientific and creative discussions as the owners explored contemporary thinking.

Later Bonnie Prince Charlie visited and gifted the Jacobite rose to the estate. It can now be found in the walled garden, close to the distillery which became operational in 2018.

And rose petals feature in the estate gin – along with juniper, coriander seeds, angelica root and citrus peel, heather pearls, pink peppercorns and sweet fennel.

The purpose-built distillery houses a specially-commissioned still from the Speyside Copper Works, meaning the gin, which was initially made elsewhere under contract, can be made on site.

Distilled by hand in batches of 600 bottles, House of Elrick Gin is also bottled at Navy strength.

The distillery is part of a regeneration plan for the Elrick estate, which will see the rennovation of the house and its listed walled garden and the creation of a tourist destination.

Distillery founder, Stuart Ingram – like previous owners of Elrick – has explored the latest ideas as he guides the estate forward.

He had initially pitched his business on the entrepreneurial TV show *Dragons' Den* but did not conclude the deal. He subsequently turned to crowdfunding for investment.

A recent innovation, however, looks back to the 17th century as it is a pair of Old Tom gins based on the core House of Elrick botanicals.

ICE & FIRE DISTILLERY

[Caithness Gin, Crofter's Tears]

Smerral, Caithness
www.iceandfiredistillery.com
First gin: July 2018

Crofting in the Highlands takes a certain strength of character. Many crofters hold down a number of jobs in addition to tending to their crops and livestock.

And in the past income might have been supplemented from distilling illicit whisky – particularly in the remote lands of Caithness.

For the Black family, crofting is part of their DNA so when a new string to their bow was needed, distilling always had to be an option.

When Iain Black, a crofter and gamekeeper, was diagnosed with cancer, it was gin that they realised could give him a different lifestyle.

He and his sister Jacqueline and their partners set up Ice & Fire Distillery in a shed on the croft.

There are two 200-litre Hoga copper pot stills from Spain, with more on their way, and after training at Strathearn Distillery, they launched their hand-crafted gins at the county show.

They pick as many wild botanicals as they can and grow their own, with some of them sheltered from the biting Caithness wind in polytunnels.

For Crofter's Tears, the hero ingredient – purple heather tips – is picked from the moors, while the rhubarb for Caithness Highland Gin comes from the croft garden.

They also use Caithness juniper which was initially located when Stephen Wright found bushes while he was rock climbing on the nearby cliffs.

With two gins – and a rum – in production, Iain is developing further recipes with his wife Eilidh, while his sister Elizabeth is working on follow-up products such as chocolates, marmalade and candles.

ILLICIT SPIRITS
[Illicit Gin]

Tradeston, Glasgow
www.illicitspirits.co.uk
First gin: April 2018

There is a gritty romance about railway arches and the industrial enterprises which operate from them, unseen by the commuters who use the trains trundling above.

One railway arch just south of the River Clyde in the centre of Glasgow makes the perfect home for Illicit Spirits, the urban craft distillery set up in 2017 by Darran Edmond.

On his Portuguese copper pot still, the Heriot-Watt alumni's first gin was a traditional London Dry-style with ten botanicals including juniper, cinnamon, coriander, angelica, orris root, orange peel and clove.

It was quickly followed by a modern take on an Old Tom. Illicit New Tom's juniper, pink peppercorns, tonka beans, rosehips and nasturtium flowers are distilled and then sweetened with Scottish blossom honey and bee pollen.

Darran calls on experience gained across Scotland's gin industry – and since botanicals lured him away from his initial intention to distil whisky.

His interest in innovation and experimentation has already led him into collaborations to create new gins.

And there was time to bottle Illicit Christmas Spirit for the festive season.

INSHRIACH DISTILLERY

Aviemore, Inverness-shire
www.inshriachgin.com
First gin: November 2014

Distiller Walter Micklethwait's imagination knows no bounds. His sauna-in-a-horsebox and firetruck campervan mean it is no surprise that his distillery is in a former chicken shed. In fact, Walter's distillery won the crown in the Channel 4 Shed of the Year Awards in 2015.

The home for his still – Little Nellie – is an eclectic mix of the Wild West and retro Scottish. The bottling room is a cosy larch-clad space where a stable once stood.

The distillery sits in a 200-acre estate of natural woodland and pasture beside the Spey and foothills of the Cairngorms.

At the heart of the estate is Inshriach House, which was built as a shooting lodge in 1906 by a Glasgow publishing family, and bought by Walter's grandfather in the 1970s.

The distillery was initially home to Crossbill, with Inshriach Gin in production since 2017.

The refreshing signature gin has an underlying fruitiness and is rounded enough to drink neat. There are juniper berries and shoots, Douglas fir and rosehip among its botanicals along with water from the estate. There is also a Navy strength version.

Using handpicked local botanicals fits with Walter's outlook on life and sustainability, but it does mean that his gin is in tune with the seasons.

For instance, the juniper harvested after the glorious summer of 2018 is quite different from what was picked in 2017. This is one of the delights of making small-batch hand-crafted gin.

As an inveterate inventor, Walker has relished the opportunity to work with other makers on creating their own gins and has distilled for Fidra and Duncan's.

The distillery is not generally open to visitors but look out for lively open days with food, music and guest gins.

ISLE OF HARRIS DISTILLERS

[Isle of Harris Gin]

Tarbert, Harris
www.harrisdistillery.com
First gin: September 2015
Tours available

For what is "first and foremost" a whisky distillery, Isle of Harris has done very well in the gin stakes.

Named the Scottish Gin Awards' Distillery of the Year in 2018, Isle of Harris has combined a social conscience with a critically-acclaimed gin.

The Hebridean distillery was the brainchild of Anderson Bakewell who wanted to address issues surrounding a fragile economy and a declining population.

And already it is having an impact: a thriving enterprise, a stream of visitors plus employment for 28 island residents all contribute to the local economy.

It doesn't stop there: the spent barley from this the first legal distillery in Harris is given to the crofters to feed their cattle.

Sugar kelp is the Isle of Harris Gin's key botanical. Lewis Mackenzie dives deep to the underwater forests of the Outer Hebrides to harvest it, careful to do so in a sustainable manner.

The dried sugar kelp is combined with juniper, coriander, angelica root, orris root, cubebs, bitter orange peel, liquorice and cassia bark to create a fresh, smooth and complex gin.

The magic takes place in a Frilli copper still called the Dottach after a Harris woman who was also fiery and feisty.

Unlike many gin makers, the Harris distillers use only the heart of the spirit run and discard, instead of recycling, the heads and tails.

The attention to detail doesn't stop there. The gin is presented in an aquamarine glass bottle – ribbed and rippled like the sands of Luskentyre – with a label hand-flecked with copper leaf and sugar kelp.

By only selling directly from the distillery (an online order can be picked up on the mainland) more of the gin's income stays in the community.

The whisky – the Hearach single malt – won't be bottled for a while yet but expect something special.

ISLE OF SKYE DISTILLERS

[Misty Isle Gin, Tommy's Gin]

Portree, Skye
www.isleofskyedistillers.com
First gin: February 2017
Gin school

It was two brothers who set up the first gin distillery on Skye in 2016. Not only have Thomas and Alistair Wilson created two signature gins – Misty Isle and Tommy's – which capture the spirit of the island, but they are now sharing the experience with students at their gin school.

Opened in the late summer of 2018, the school is at the distillery shop in the centre of Portree.

Meanwhile, the brothers create their own gins on the outskirts of the town. With four pot stills, the purpose-built distillery allows the Wilsons to combine the spring waters from the Storr Lochs with their botanicals, some of which they grow on site.

Inspired by Skye's dramatic landscape, Misty Isle Gin uses juniper berries foraged from the hills and its 11 botanicals include a top secret ingredient which only comes from the island.

Its other botanicals include coriander, grains of paradise, orris root, liquorice root, black cubebs, angelica root, lemon verbena, lemon peel and cassia bark.

The result is a juniper-heavy gin with earthy undertones, a hint of spice and citrus flavours.

Tommy's is a poignant tribute to the brothers' late father, Tommy, who served in the army, and all soldiers – or Tommies.

For Thomas, who himself served in the Parachute Regiment, it is a matter of pride that for every bottle sold, a donation is made to military charities.

The gin uses juniper from Tommy's sister Fay's farm in Croatia.

Bottled at 45% ABV, it also includes poppy seeds, coriander, liquorice root, blaeberry and sweet orange – and drinks quite differently from Misty Isle.

Both gins are presented in distinctive bottles which capture their provenance. Misty Isle's label shows the Black Cuillin, while Tommy's is inspired by the Commando memorial at Spean Bridge, near Fort William.

KELSO GIN COMPANY

[The Crow Man's, Kelso Elephant, Lovage]

Ancrum, Roxburghshire
kelsoginco.com
First gin: December 2016

Folklore tells of medicine men who toured the countryside with tinctures and potions of herbs, spices and secret ingredients to restore the sick and ailing.

In the Borders, they tell of one of these travellers who wore a mask with a large "nose" filled with herbs and spices to ward off disease. They called him the Crow Man.

It was almost inevitable that when Oliver Drake and Robert Armstrong were looking for a name for Kelso Gin Company's core product they should consider the legendary figure who created reviving drinks.

The Crow Man's Gin uses organic grain spirit for a smooth classic juniper-led gin with subtle tones of cinnamon. Like the wandering Crow Man, the Kelso team keeps some of the ingredients a secret.

Kelso's larger-than-life Elephant Gin is strong on flavour from its mix of oriental spices and local botanicals. But it is also inspired by the legend that an elephant is buried under Kelso Square.

Lovage Gin uses its namesake herb alongside olives and orange zest for an intriguing fresh taste.

In real life, Robert is a fourth generation distiller and his gins reflect the seasons using ingredients foraged locally.

The distillery is located alongside other craft businesses at Harestanes and is home to two Portuguese 200-litre copper stills called Penny and Tuppence and an upstairs bottling room.

Here the hand-printed labels are applied to the small batches in the range which includes fruit flavours, as well as a bourbon-cask aged Reiver Spirit and Wojciech Vodka.

KINRARA DISTILLERY

[Kinrara Highland Dry Gin]

Aviemore, Inverness-shire
www.kinraradistillery.com
First gin: March 2018

The special landscape of the Cairngorms National Park is host to rare flora, fauna and wildlife, as well as four of the UK's five highest mountains and 55 Munros.

The estates in the park encapsulate that environment and give a wealth of inspiration for gin makers.

At Kinrara, there are berries to forage, pure water to distil with and inspiration for designers.

Kinrara's distillery is in a 250-year-old farm steading and it is making handcrafted small-batch gins using its handmade traditional alembic copper pot stills.

The gins are developed on Wee Alice, a 50-litre Hoga still, before moving into production on the 100-litre stills.

The distillery's signature Kinrara Highland Dry Gin uses rowanberries and rosehips foraged from the estate alongside eight traditional botanicals and water filtered through the hills.

Drinking the gin, the foraged botanicals give way to a long subtle orange and juniper finish.

The area's visual beauty is being showcased in its limited release Artist Edition gins.

The first releases featured the work of Kat Baxter from Dundee. She used a mixture of pen, pencil and paint in her delightful botanical-inspired illustrations of Highland animals.

At specialist glass decorator, Seaways Services, organic inks and transfers were used in the process to bake the enamel into the bottle making them real collectors' items.

Meanwhile, the creativity of the distiller David Wilson is being captured in the estate editions – the first of which was a Hibiscus Gin made with cold compounded hibiscus flowers and sweet orange peel.

He is also busy with the distillery's plans to make single malt whisky to lay down.

LANGSTANE LIQUOR COMPANY

[Porter's Gin]

Aberdeen
www.portersgin.co.uk
First gin: December 2015
Tours available

In the basement of the Orchid, a popular Aberdeen cocktail bar, is one of Scotland's most intriguing distilleries.

The home of Porter's Gin has been created around the ability to distil botanicals at low temperatures.

The technique captures the bright fresh notes and preserves the natural flavours and fragrant aromas of the ingredients.

Founders Alex Lawrence, Ben Iravani and Josh Rennie took a long road to creating their bespoke distilling environment, with the first experiments done on a homemade rotavap.

Perfecting the Porter's recipe which uses 12 ethically-sourced botanicals was what can only be described as an adventure in research and experimentation.

For instance, when the trio decided to use the rare Asian citrus fruit, Buddha's hand, they ended up going directly to Chinese farmers who grow and dry it – and in turn became one of its largest importers in Europe.

They use a combination of modern and traditional techniques, distilling some botanicals in the Orchid's three vacuum stills and having others distilled in a British wheat base spirit in a copper pot-still at G&J Distillers in Cheshire.

They used the same approach to create Porter's Tropical Old Tom – again staying true to the classic combination of sweetened gin and exotic botanicals, but employing cold distillation to add the passion fruit, guava and white tea flavours.

LILLIARD GINNERY

[Lilliard]

Lanton Mill, Roxburghshire
lilliardgin.co.uk
First gin: February 2017
Tours available

The still beside the River Teviot might be one of the smallest in Scotland, but it is born of big inspiration.

Donald, the tiny 60-litre copper still, is producing a gin named after one of the larger-than-life characters in Borders folklore, Lilliard.

Her heroics were fighting to the death against the English in 1545 at the Battle of Ancrum Moor.

Distilled just across the river from the scene of the battle, Lilliard captures the seasons of the area.

The botanicals – including rowan, rosehip, meadowsweet, elderflower, angelica, liquorice root and juniper – elegantly evoke the landscape in the floral gin.

The ginnery was founded by Kate Macinnes who, after two decades working in financial services, wanted to make something she loved.

Its next door neighbour is Born in the Borders, the visitor centre between Jedburgh and Denholm where local produce takes pride of place.

The businesses share the lush Teviot valley with otters, red squirrels and ospreys attracted by the abundance of salmon in the river.

LINLITHGOW DISTILLERY
[LinGin]

Linlithgow, West Lothian
www.linlithgowdistillery.co.uk
First gin: January 2018

LinGin takes the concept of a local product to new levels. Everything has been designed around its birthplace, the royal burgh of Linlithgow.

First, there is the revival of the distilling tradition of the town which at one time had five whisky distilleries.

Then, there is the tasting panel of 119 residents who helped Alyson and Ross Jamieson create the recipe for LinGin.

It, in turn, uses botanicals foraged around the town – beside the loch and canal – and is made on a stainless steel still called Gleann Iucha (the Gaelic for Linlithgow).

Finally there is the bottle: shaped like one of the town's most recognisable landmarks – the old tower and modern spire of St Michael's Church beside the royal palace.

What makes the London Dry-style gin special is the meadowsweet they forage from the banks of the Union Canal.

Combined with juniper, coriander, cassia, angelica, orris root, bitter orange, cardamom, cubeb berries and three other secret botanicals, LinGin has both spicy and citrus notes.

As Alyson explains: "The experience should evoke memories of a stroll along the canal or round the loch on a warm summer evening and leave you looking for more."

Alyson and Ross, who had both worked in IT for many years, have obviously put a lot of thought into their product, keen to give it real provenance.

With the gin launched, 2018 saw them busy renovating and moving into their new distillery, ready to welcome visitors.

They also found time to develop the first of their Four Mary's special editions.

LOCH NESS SPIRITS

[Loch Ness Gin]

Dores, Inverness-shire
wearelochness.com
First gin: August 2016

When you have native juniper growing on your doorstep, it must be tempting to make gin.

In fact, when Lorien and Kevin Cameron-Ross heard that most of the juniper used in Scottish gin had to be imported from eastern Europe and Italy, they even thought about picking it commercially.

Instead, Lorien, a doctor and Kevin, a retired detective, started on a journey which led to the creation of Loch Ness Spirits.

On the way, they distilled everything they could pick from their land, experimenting with flavours and combinations.

Kevin did training, they navigated red tape and created a distillery in an old stable which now houses three stills – two copper and a high-tech 500-litre still.

They have a growing portfolio of spirits, but it all started with Loch Ness Gin made with their handpicked juniper and the pure Highland water which flows into the loch.

The gin's exact botanicals are not revealed but all grow close to their home. This secrecy is rather fitting: the gin's dark bottle with its distinctive Nessie logo is a nod to the biggest mystery in the area.

In 2018, they launched Legends, a gin series in which each edition will be inspired by one of the myths of Loch Ness.

The first batch was a classic London Dry-style juniper-led gin, with an added creamy taste from hawthorn berries and based on the legend of the birth of Loch Ness itself.

Alongside their gin making, Lorien has created Loch Ness Absinthe Blanche. Distilled with botanicals, including juniper, aniseed, wormwood and fennel, it quickly won a gold medal at awards in the absinthe heartland of France.

LONE WOLF DISTILLERY

[Lone Wolf Gin]

Ellon, Aberdeenshire
www.lonewolfspirits.com
First gin: April 2017

BrewDog has a reputation for doing things differently. James Watt and Martin Dickie shook up the brewing world when they started crafting beer in 2007 and then the corporate sector when they pioneered crowdfunding with their Equity for Punks. It's no surprise then that their distillery is blazing its own trail – as a grain-to-glass operation.

Using the barley and wheat mash from the BrewDog brewery, the distillation starts in a triple bubble still before it encounters an 18-metre 60-plate rectification column.

Designed by head of distillation, Steven Kersley, with German engineering company Arnold Holstein, the unusual bubble still means the spirit has a large amount of contact with the copper.

The result of extensive research – and 192 unique distillations – Lone Wolf Gin brings together 14 botanicals.

The headliners are Scots pine, kaffir lime leaf, Thai lemongrass, lavender flower and two fresh citrus peels and they mean lots of character around the gin's juniper core.

With Lone Wolf Gin and Vodka established, Steven has continued to experiment and push the boundaries. A small-batch release at Navy strength, Gunpowder Gin, fires a blast of Oriental peppery spice over a wave of citrus.

LOST LOCH SPIRITS DISTILLERY

Dess, Aberdeenshire
www.lostlochspirits.com

[EeNoo Gin]

First gin: February 2017

Ask an Aberdonian when is it time for gin, and they'll fire back "eenoo". It's not surprising, as in old Scots "eenoo" means "just now" and, as we all know, it's always time for gin.

EeNoo Gin therefore couldn't come from anywhere other than Aberdeenshire. In fact, it was Royal Deeside's long history of distilling – with both commercial distilleries and a tradition of smuggling and home stills – which inspired Peter Dignan and Richard Pierce to set up Lost Loch Spirits near Aboyne in 2017.

The distillery sits between forest and farmland on the edge of the Cairngorm National Park. Its "lost loch" was Loch Auchlossan, which was drained to make way for crops in the Second World War.

Their gin is distilled with Royal Deeside honey which takes its flavours from the heather, willow herb and clover that the bees feed off.

Humans harvest the botanicals – the berries from the countryside around the distillery or farms in Aberdeenshire and Angus, while the juniper comes from the Italian highlands

EeNoo's botanicals include heather flowers, brambleberries, raspberries, rosehip, coriander seeds, angelica root, liquorice root, orange and lemon peel which together with the honey create a traditional yet smooth, fruity gin.

Its label pays tribute to Eenoolooapik, an Inuit who visited Aberdeenshire in the 1800s and shared his knowledge of herbs, spices and botanicals, picking up the nickname Eenoo.

Proud to be a part of a legal, modern-day resurgence of craft distilling, Pete and Rich have both a modern iStill and a traditional copper alembic still with which to make 80,000 bottles of spirits a year.

Thinking of the future, they use a biomass boiler, wind and solar energy to help power their production.

Lost Loch Spirits' products don't stop at gin: the range includes Haroosh – a traditional infusion of brambleberries and honey and whisky – and Scotland's first absinthe, Murmichan.

LUNDIN DISTILLING

[Gorse Gin]

Kirkcaldy, Fife
www.lundindistilling.com
First gin: December 2017

In Scotland, golfers and gorse are often found in close proximity. The prickly bush with its bright yellow flowers is a feature of many golf courses.

After a round of golf, Iain Brown was contemplating his form and finding solace in the incredible aroma of the gorse in full bloom which had been the backdrop for his round at Lundin Golf Club. It was then that he hit on the idea of using gorse in a gin and Lundin Distilling was born.

Although he had worked in Edinburgh as a lawyer, Iain always knew he wanted to return to Fife where his grandfathers had been publicans and his father worked for Diageo. Setting up a distillery in the kingdom was not really a surprising move. He had help in the form of an experienced distiller who has worked for leading brands. "On the basis of my ideas and his expertise, we refined Gorse Gin," he says.

Iain turned to the US for his still where the craft distilling scene means still-makers design for artisan distillers. "There's not a touch-screen in

sight. It may be old school but there's a real sense of connection when you're having to physically turn valves and listen to the still to ensure you're bringing across the very best product," he adds.

The London Dry-style gin has 18 botanicals including two types of juniper, elderflower, chamomile, caraway, grapefruit, bitter orange and cinnamon beside the gorse. The gorse is handpicked from around Lundin GC's links course and adds almond and vanilla notes as well as an unexpected peppery warmth.

In the future, there will probably be some limited editions of Gorse and the idea of showing off the still to visitors is under consideration but, for the moment, Iain's focus is on his signature gin.

LUSSA DRINKS COMPANY

[Lussa Gin]

Ardlussa, Jura
www.lussagin.com
First gin: August 2016
Tours available

The weather is unforgiving, the landscape tough and making gin on Jura is only for the adventurous. But Alicia Macinnes, Claire Fletcher and Georgina Kitching were up for the challenge and are now thriving on it.

Their distillery is in former stables on the 16,000-acre Ardlussa estate in the north of the island and almost as far from the ferry to Islay as you can go.

Their gin captures the essence of the Inner Hebridean island using 15 botanicals that can grow there. The list includes lemon thyme, coriander seed, rose petals, elderflower, ground elder, rosehip, bog myrtle, Scots pine, lemon balm, orris root, honeysuckle, sea lettuce, water mint, lime tree flowers and juniper.

They gather them from the hills, glens, lochs, bogs and the sea or grow them in their gardens and polytunnels.

The botanicals they can't grow enough of (yet), they buy in and they have been busy propagating Jura juniper and nurturing Argyll-grown juniper towards its first harvest in 2022.

Lussa Gin is now made in a Portuguese 200-litre copper alembic still called Hamish, having started out with Jim, a 10-litre still in a kitchen. It is bottled by the trio on the island.

Unsurprisingly, the friends wanted a taste of summer in their gin and its citrus notes come from the lemon thyme and lemon balm.

The aromatic watermint, bog myrtle and Scots pine are balanced with a savoury kick from ground elder and sea lettuce.

Honeysuckle adds sweetness and rose petals and rosehip give a smoothness that is a world away from the landscape that made it.

MORAY DISTILLERY

[Avva Scottish Gin]

Elgin, Moray
moraydistilleryltd.co.uk
First gin: October 2016

In a world where we often think bigger is better, Moray Distillery proves good things come in small packages.

Founded by Jill Brown, the gin distillery has what is probably the smallest still in Speyside – and it was made just a short distance away.

The bespoke copper still was made by Speyside Copper Works in Elgin and LH Stainless of Keith. For short, the still is known as J-J – after Jill's grandmothers Jessie and Jean.

When it came to finding a name for her gin, she went further afield but still kept a sense of those close to her. In the Indian language of Dravidian, Avva means a respected older woman in the family. It also means "to ruin" in Hebrew so there is a neat link to gin's past notoriety as mother's ruin.

When it came to choosing the 11 botanicals for Avva Scottish Gin, five – rowan, red clover, mint, dandelion and nettle – are sourced just a small distance from home.

And in the making, Avva is distilled in small batches, bottled, numbered and signed by the distiller.

Avva is bottled at 43% and Navy strength 57.2% ABV. There is also a six-month bourbon cask matured 55% edition.

Inspiration for the label came from something – again – close at hand: Elgin Cathedral.

Pocket Rocket Creative's design evokes a rose window which might have existed above the entrance before the church was abandoned at the time of the Scottish Reformation.

Avva might have small origins and close-to-home credentials, but Avva is a gin with a big juniper kick and clear citrus finish.

NB DISTILLERY

[NB Gin]

North Berwick, East Lothian
nbdistillery.com
First gin: October 2013
Tours available

East Lothian is one of Scotland's most fertile counties. Rich farmland, lush countryside and bountiful waters mean its reputation as a food and drink destination is second to none.

The NB Distillery is one of its newest attractions.

More than four years after launching NB Gin, the purpose-built eco-friendly distillery opened on the outskirts of the pretty fishing town which gives the gin its name.

The London Dry-style gin has made quite an impact in those years with it picking up awards, finding export markets and being served at top events including the Queen's 90th birthday celebrations.

It is an impressive record for something which was initially developed with a pressure cooker and central heating pipes on the kitchen table of two lawyers, Vivienne and Steve Muir.

After much research, they found a recipe which matched their idea of a perfect gin and they launched their company.

They had a still made to their specifications and started making the classic eight-botanical gin in a unit in the town.

As sales grew – especially overseas – and they expanded their product range, Viv and Steve started to plan the new distillery which opened to visitors in April 2018.

Alongside their original John Dore gin still, they have a bespoke Jamaican-style copper double retort still which they use to make rum.

NB Gin lines up beside NB Navy strength, a rum, citrus vodka and NB Samphire, a contemporary style London Dry with notes of ginger, lemon and green tea.

OLD CURIOSITY DISTILLERY

[Secret Garden Gins]

Lothianburn, Midlothian
www.theoldcuriosity.co.uk
First gin: October 2017
Tours available

For Hamish Martin, the roots of his distillery are his plants. A former wine merchant, Hamish had fallen in love with a one-time organic market garden in the Pentland Hills, on the southern outskirts of Edinburgh.

Rashly buying the land in 2011, then building a house for him and his wife, Liberty, to live in with their children, Hamish created the Secret Herb Garden.

With more than 600 naturally grown herbs, a shop and café, the garden is a plant paradise and supplies many of the capital's top restaurants with fresh ingredients.

Hamish, who had a long-standing passion for plants, has spent many hours studying herbology and learning from experts in the field.

As he made tinctures from the plants he was growing, Hamish noted how adding tonic to his rose distillate had a magical effect.

It was what is known as "cabbage juice chemistry" where a water-soluble pigment changes colour when its PH levels are altered.

It was an intriguing idea to translate into a gin. The three Secret Garden Gins – Apothecary Rose, Lavender & Echinacea and Chamomile & Cornflower – all naturally change colour when mixed with tonic. In the case of the rose gin, it is from sepia to vibrant pink.

Unsurprisingly for such a unique product, Marks & Spencer quickly teamed up with Hamish to launch its own brand colour-changing gins.

The Old Curiosity Distillery sits in a corner of the herb garden, close to the floral botanicals which the team pick and dry on site.

The quantity of gin it can make is determined by the each year's harvest. Consequently, limited editions – such as 2018's Damask Rose – can be just 400 bottles.

Hamish has also planted more than 500 juniper cuttings so that ultimately he can use the garden's own juniper in its gins.

OLD POISON DISTILLERY

[Selkie Gin]

Leith, Edinburgh
www.oldpoison.co.uk
First gin: January 2018

Fabrizio Cioffi pours his Italian passion into his approach to drinks. As a mixologist, Fabrizio understands how flavours work together and what consumers will love.

After years working in London bars, a move to Edinburgh for the opening of the Refinery in St Andrew Square gave him a less frenetic pace of life – and the time to follow his entrepreneurial dream.

He set about creating a distillery. Located in the Biscuit Factory in Leith he has a 30-litre copper pot still called Aurora, bottling kit and the paraphernalia to make cocktail bitters.

It might be an urban industrial unit, but it doesn't dampen Fabrizio's passion and his signature gin is inspired by his hometown of Naples where lemons and limes ripen in the sun.

It's a fresh citrus London Dry-style gin which works just as well for bartenders as it does at home.

When it came to a name for his gin, Fabrizio has turned to the country which has seduced him and he now calls home.

Orcadian folklore says the Selkie can change from a seal to a human with magical seductive powers. Fabrizio hopes his Selkie Gins will seduce those that taste it.

ORKNEY DISTILLERY

[Kirkjuvagr, Arkh-Angell, Harpa, Aurora]

Kirkwall, Orkney
www.orkneydistilling.com
First gin: August 2016
Tours available

Orkney has been a destination for travellers for many centuries. Today more than 140 cruise ships carrying in the region of 125,000 passengers call at Kirkwall each year. Greeting them on the harbourside since the summer of 2018 is the Orkney Distillery. With a coffee and gin bar, shop and the micro distillery, it is proving a popular destination and brings valuable jobs to the community. Built by Stephen and Aly Kemp to house their gin-making operations, this stylish contemporary space allows visitors to learn – as well as taste the distillery's gins.

The gins – Kirkjuvagr, Arkh-Angell, Harpa and Aurora – are infused with the islands' Norse heritage. Kirkjuvagr was what the Vikings called Kirkwall. Like now, it was an important port for the seafarers who would sail their longships into "Church Bay". Arkh-Angell is a "storm" – or Navy – strength edition of it launched in 2017.

Developed with support from the University of the Highlands & Islands and Strathearn Distillery, the Kemps' recipe for Kirkjuvagr built on the legend that the wild angelica growing on the islands was originally taken to Orkney by Viking sailors.

With this angelica they blend other botanicals found on the islands – Ramanas rose, Burnet rose and borage – and Orkney bere barley.

The Orcadian botanicals are grown for them near Kirkwall by the university's Agronomy Institute.

Keeping to the Norse theme, further seasonal Orkney gins have been launched.

The lighter, sweeter Harpa is for the summer, while Aurora celebrates the Northern Lights with the addition of cinnamon, nutmeg, cloves and pink and black peppercorns.

THE PENTLAND STILL

[King's Hill Gin]

Loanhead, Midlothian
www.kingshillgin.com
First gin: July 2018

The spot where Sandy Morrison forages his botanicals is redolent with history. Not only is it on ancient volcanic hills scattered with archaeological remains, but it is the legendary site of a royal wager.

King's Hill Gin takes its name from a bet between King Robert the Bruce and Sir William Sinclair of Roslin.

The wager – to catch a white stag that roamed the king's estate in the Pentland hills – was won by Sinclair. When the king congratulated him, Sinclair, who also won the estate, named the spot King's Hill.

It was here that Sandy realised that the Pentlands have a wealth of botanicals – from brambles, sloes, heather, gorse and elderflower to rosehips, rowan, crab apples and even a few patches of juniper.

A keen hillwalker, Sandy is also a gin fan and he realised he could make something glorious out of the abundance of botanicals right on his door step.

In King's Hill, Sandy has created a juniper-led, crisp and clear London Dry gin, entirely hand-crafted from hill to bottle. Its other key botanicals are rosehip, heather, gorse and elderflower.

Made in Marion, a traditional Iberian copper pot still, the gin is presented in stylish glass bottles.

The 12 lines on the bottles represent the 12 botanicals used in creating the gin, as well as being the outlines of the hills of the Pentlands. The stag's antlers crown the gin's initials.

PERSIE DISTILLERY

[Persie Gins]

Glenshee, Perthshire
www.persiedistillery.com
First gin: April 2016
Tours available

The sense of smell is just as important as taste when it comes to enjoying gin.

This was something Simon and Chrissie Fairclough saw at first hand as they toured the country with a car load of gins, running tasting sessions as Gin Club Scotland.

They noted that three styles – fruity, savoury and sweet – were consistently the most popular and that the top-scoring gins had more than a nice taste – they had aroma. The Fairacloughs' touring gin club proved to be invaluable market research.

When it came to making their own gin, they knew they wanted to make gins which smelled good in those three styles. So, their trio are: Zesty Citrus Gin, Herby & Aromatic Gin and Sweet & Nutty Old Tom.

Of course, they needed gin-making skills and a distillery to make them in. In 2013, Simon gained his qualification from the Institute of Brewing & Distilling and they bought the former Persie Hotel at the foot of Glenshee, where they have created a distillery and visitor centre in a former steading.

They make small batches of Persie Gin in a bespoke, 230-litre copper pot still, called Phil, using local glen water.

Each gin has botanicals carefully chosen to evoke an emotive and comforting scent: sharp citrus for the fruity gin, fresh herbs for the savoury gin and almonds and vanilla pods for the sweet gin.

PIXEL SPIRITS
[Devil's Staircase, Neptune's Staircase]

North Ballachulish, Lochaber
www.pixelspiritsltd.co.uk
First gin: October 2017
Gin school

The hunt for a bespoke gin for their hotel led West Coast hoteliers into an adventure they could never have imagined.

Now Craig and Noru Innes have their own distillery, an award-winning gin and a gin school.

The owners of the Loch Leven Hotel were looking for a gin that would suit guests when they come in from enjoying the countryside – probably after walking or climbing.

Named after a nearby section of the West Highland Way, Devil's Staircase is a spiced gin with warm notes of cardamom, cassia, grains of paradise and nutmeg – the ideal welcome after a day in the hills.

The label is a design by Iain McIntosh, who is probably best known for his illustrations for books by Alexander McCall Smith.

The outdoors theme was evident when they made Neptune's Staircase Gin. It celebrates the impressive run of lochs on the Caledonian Canal near Fort William with fresh notes of nettle and seaweed.

The distillery itself has been converted from 17th-century byres on land beside the hotel. The conversion work was done mostly by Craig and friends and family.

It is very much an artisan operation with batches of less than 80 bottles filled and labelled by hand.

Keeping things small and personal, the gin school's make-your-own classes are limited to eight people at a time.

PRÀBAN NA LINNE
[Uisge Lusach – The Gaelic Gin]

Sleat, Skye
www.gaelicwhisky.com
First gin: December 2017
Tours available

The era of illicit stills hidden away in remote glens across the Highlands and Islands is long gone. Today's craft distillers make no secret of their endeavours.

On the Eilean Iarmain estate overlooking the Sound of Sleat, a small still is now making legal Gaelic gin under the direction of head distiller Leah Dunlop.

The traditional copper still is said to be identical to the smugglers' stills and small enough to be carried around on horseback. Its cooling worm is housed in an old whisky cask and a botanical infusing basket has been added to the copper lyne arm.

Uisge Lusach – probably best translated as "herbaceous spirit" – uses Skye's soft water and botanicals gathered from the hills, moors and woodlands of the estate. Its juniper is balanced by a bright lemon citrus and delicate warming spice. Leah also gathers fruit and flowers close to the distillery for a growing range of small-batch gin liqueurs.

Pràban na Linne is part of the legacy of the entrepreneur Sir Iain Nobel who wanted to bring a greater understanding and appreciation of Scotland's Gaelic heritage and its relevance in economic development.

It is the producer of the Gaelic Whiskies which was established in 1976 to provide authentic whisky for Gaelic-speaking connoisseurs in the Hebrides.

Before that Sir Iain had founded Sabhal Mòr Ostaig, the Gaelic University College of Scotland.

Another part of his legacy was one of Scotland's first native woodland regeneration schemes.

Fortuitously, native juniper was included in the regeneration and planting schemes for the Sleat woodland. And juniper from there makes up some of the quantity needed for Uisge Lusach.

ROGUE DISTILLERY

[Felons]

St Andrews, Fife
www.felons-gin.com
First gin: April 2018

Almost the last place you would expect to find a distillery is at the back of a popular restaurant.

For Kained Holdings, which has bars and restaurants across Scotland, innovation is nothing new.

The three friends behind Kained, who have many years of experience in the hospitality sector between them, saw their customers were confused by the number of gins on the market.

They realised it was time to create a no-nonsense full-flavour citrus gin.

When they took over an old St Andrews pub, they had the opportunity to install a custom-built 100-litre still during the renovations of what is now Rogue restaurant and bar.

Under the watchful eye of distiller Fraser Barrett, Felons gin takes its citrus aromas from angelica seeds, lemon verbena and bitter orange peel. There are subtle floral notes from orris root, sweet almond and cubeb berries.

Fraser was the ideal fit when the team at Kained was looking for a distiller to set up the Rogue micro distillery.

With experience of the drinks industry from bartending, management and consultancy, he had then gone to Glasgow to study biological science with his sights set on moving into brewing or distilling.

After a period at the Glasgow Distillery, Fraser joined the Rogue team.

SAXA VORD DISTILLERY

[Shetland Reel Gin, Ocean Scent, Simmer Dim]

Unst, Shetland
www.shetlandreel.com
First gin: November 2014
Tours available

Adapting to economic change has been a feature of life in Scotland over the years. It is never easy, but Scots are adaptable and innovative and in the Northern Isles there is plenty of evidence of this.

On the Shetland island of Unst, when the RAF Saxa Vord radar base closed in 2006 it was an opportunity to redevelop the support site as a holiday resort.

Frank and Debbie Strang's vision was to give this wild, beautiful and remote place an economic lifeline. Tourism alone would not be enough, however, and soon they teamed up with Stuart and Wilma Nickerson to create the Shetland Distillery Company. They planned a distillery in a former supply building which would lead to more permanent jobs.

Stuart brings a wealth of experience from the whisky industry where he worked for some of the best-known distilleries, so ultimately Saxa Vord will make whisky but first came the gin.

Shetland Reel Original Gin uses nine botanicals including apple mint grown at Unst Market Garden for a well-balanced London Dry.

This was followed by Ocean Scent with bladderwrack seaweed as its local hero – and the islands' seagoing heritage as inspiration.

The midnight sun is another feature of Shetland and the long summer twilight is known as the Simmer Dim. It was the inspiration for a summery third gin.

A Shetland distillery couldn't let the spectacular Up Helly Aa fire festival pass without a dramatic product. Each year Saxa Vord has created a cask-aged Navy strength gin for the celebrations.

These gins line up with a Lidl exclusive, fruit liqueur and blended malt whiskies.

SELKIRK DISTILLERS

[Reiver's and Bannock gins]

Selkirk, Selkirkshire
www.selkirkdistillers.com
First gin: September 2017

The Borders were once lawless lands caught between the auld enemies of England and Scotland. To survive the climate of fear that these wars generated, Borderers became Reivers – cattle and sheep rustlers and raiders. They fought dirty but are admired for their skills and loyalty to their clans.

Reiver's gin was conceived in the heart of the Borders by two couples from Selkirk, Allan & Jane Walker and Dave & Susan Myatt. Using the flowers of the gorse which give the rich yellow covering to the Selkirkshire hillsides, they created a gin described as "bold juniper, subtle citrus and a hint of floral". Keeping true to their location, the distillers commissioned Conor McAllister, who was born in the town, to design their distinctive labels.

Today, one of Selkirk's best known products is the Selkirk Bannock. It is a fruit bread: not something that necessarily comes to mind when we think of gin. But that didn't stop the Selkirk Distillers.

Using bannocks from Camerons bakery on the High Street and macerating them in juniper gin for about a month, a fruity "bannock in a bottle" gin was the result.

Initially distilled at Strathearn Distillery in Perthshire, Reiver's and Bannock now have their own home.

The still arrived in Selkirk from Portugal in late 2018 and in future Selkirk Distillers' gin will be produced at its new home in the old joinery on the Philiphaugh estate.

Limited editions have included two military-inspired creations. From 1914 to 1918, 1,296 young men left the royal burgh of Selkirk to go to war. To commemorate the lives of the 292 who failed to return, 292 specially-designed bottles of Reiver's Gin have been released.

The RAF100 edition of Reiver's marks the centenary of the founding of the Royal Air Force in 2018 and will have raised £300 for the RAF Benevolent Fund.

SOLWAY SPIRITS

[Solway Gins]

Cummertrees, Dumfriesshire
www.solwayspirits.co.uk
First gin: autumn 2016

People get into gin in different ways. For Andrew Emmerson he comes from the real ale scene. He set up Andrews Ales in 2011 using traditional techniques to brew real ale and make cider from apples gathered close to the village which is near Annan on the Solway Firth.

At Solway Sprits which he opened in 2014, Andrew makes small batches – 50 bottles at a time – of artisan spirits and liqueurs.

He started with liqueurs and the first one – Raspberry Ripple Gin Liqueur – is still one of Solway's best sellers.

Solway's gins are created using a rectification column, then bottled and labelled by hand.

The botanicals include some that are foraged in the rich Dumfriesshire countryside as well as juniper, coriander, orris root, angelica, orange peel and liquorice root.

As a result, Solway Dry Gin's juniper mellows into cumin and cardamom with citrus notes, while Solway Classic Gin is a sweeter Old Tom-style with angelica and liquorice.

Among Andrew's other creations is Rhubarb Crumble Gin where the Solway Gin is infused with rhubarb and vanilla.

Here we see a hint of Andrew's real ale roots, as he also lets it infuse briefly with torrified wheat, something you would more usually find used in brewing.

SPEYSIDE DISTILLERY

[Byron's Gin]

Kingussie, Inverness-shire
speysidedistillery.co.uk
First gin: October 2017
Tours available

An army of enthusiasts across Britain make meticulous records of its plant life. These recorders of the Botanical Society of the British Isles have enviable knowledge of the botanicals in their area.

When the owners of the Speyside Distillery wanted to create a gin, there was no-one better qualified than the BSBI's county recorder Andy Amphlett.

Andy identified suitable plants and berries from the distillery gardens and nearby, so that distillery manager Sandy Jamieson could add his technical expertise to create gin.

In Byron's Bird Cherry, lemon-scented fern, lady's bedstraw, rowan, wild thyme, juniper and blaeberry join the bird cherry as botanicals.

Meanwhile, Scot's pine, sweet vernal-grass, juniper, rowan, downy birch, aspen and melancholy thistle were used to create Byron's Melancholy Thistle.

With these unique botanicals, it is appropriate that Byron's Gin supports the next generation of botanists by making donations to the BSBI's training programme.

Both expressions of the gin are distilled in a copper pot still with integrated botanicals basket at the distillery, a 200-year-old former barley mill and croft.

The distillery is also home to SPEY whisky – a brand which dates back to the 19th century when the forefathers of today's chief executive John Harvey McDonough were also making whisky.

For the gin's name the distillery turned to one of the 19th century's most colourful figures, Lord Byron, who also happens to have spent much of his first decade in Aberdeen. Like many of the Romantic poets he loved the Scottish Highlands and he is said to have given his wedding guests a cask of malt whisky – thought to have been a SPEY.

STIRLING DISTILLERY
[Stirling Gin]

Stirling
stirlinggin.co.uk
First gin: October 2015

Stirling's latest visitor attraction is a gin distillery. The Castle and Old Town Jail already draw thousands of tourists up the hill to explore their history and now the royal burgh's gin has a new home.

Opened in the spring of 2019, the Old Smiddy houses stills, packaging and bottling lines and a visitors' centre.

June and Cameron McCann had launched Stirling Gin after running their first gin festival and realising that the city was missing its own product.

Already the owners of a bottle shop and operating the very popular Stirling Whisky Festival, the McCanns had spotted the growing interest in gin and ran that first gin festival in November 2014.

It was while walking their dog that June and Cameron grasped the potential of using the nettle that grows wild in Stirlingshire as a botanical for their gin. They researched, experimented and refined their recipe on a small copper pot still called Jinty before having the first batch made in time for their 25th wedding anniversary.

Alongside juniper, Stirling Gin also uses fresh basil, angelica, orange and lemon, and some of the botanicals they hope will grow in the garden beside their new distillery.

In preparation for the move, the McCanns launched the Folklore Collection of gin liqueurs, with the release of the raspberry Red Cap and mint and bramble Green Lady.

Ironically, the distillery building which was once a temperance hall, will allow whisky and rum to be added to the Stirling portfolio.

STRATHEARN DISTILLERY

[Strathearn Gin]

Methven, Perthshire
www.strathearndistillery.com
First gin: August 2013
Tours available

Strathearn Gin is the stepping stone to whisky for this Perthshire distillery. And, as a distillery set on doing things differently, it has created a string of innovative gins as it waited for its first malt spirit to become whisky.

The founder Tony Reeman-Clark had always been something of a trailblazer and when someone at a whisky event planted the idea of having his own distillery, he went out and made it a reality.

The distillery, on a farm in the fertile Earn valley, is home to 500- and 1,000-litre copper pot stills meaning the batches of gin are small and bottling and filling are by hand.

Strathearn's core gins use a double distillation technique involving both sizes of still. The Scottish Gin is a classic strongly juniper-led drink, with coriander, orange peel, angelica root, calamus root and grains of paradise.

Heather Rose Gin's delicate botanicals – rose petals and heather flowers – are compounded with liquorice. It is notable for changing colour when tonic is added.

Innovation has been a constant feature of the Strathearn story: there have been cask-matured and Navy strength gins and in 2016 it was first to market with a Scottish cider brandy, made in collaboration with Thistly Cross Cider.

Its whisky also went on sale in 2016, followed by Dunedin, an early Scottish rum.

The distillery's innovations, collaborations and support for other distillers has meant a pivotal role for Tony in Scotland's emerging modern craft distilling sector.

It's been quite a journey for a former IT and management consultant with a grounding in engineering.

STRATHLEVEN DISTILLERS
[Gilt Gin]

Vale of Leven, Dunbartonshire
www.strathlevendistillers.com
First gin: July 2010

As the craft spirit market was taking root in the UK, Ricky Christie set up a boutique distillery.

It was 2008 and Ricky, who has a wealth of experience gained from Speyside Distillers, which his father had owned, created it to distil premium gin and vodka from malted barley.

The copper still is specially designed to Ricky's exact specifications. There is also a bespoke chill filtration system to make sure the spirit is extra pure.

Gilt is the premium gin and its distinctive creamy smoothness is down to the five-times distilled malted barley spirit it is created from.

This single malt gin, which has notes of warm cardamom and fresh citrus, is presented in a tall elegant bottle.

The fact that people detect a hint of whisky – and often enjoy it neat – should be no surprise hearing how it is made.

STRATHMASHIE DISTILLERY

[Daffy's Gin]

Newtonmore, Inverness-shire
www.daffysgin.com
First gin: December 2014
Gin school

Legend has it that Prince Albert once danced on the table in the distillery tasting room.

It couldn't be more fitting that the distillery gin is named after the Victorian slang word for gin.

Daffy's was the brainchild of Chris Molyneaux and Mignonne Khazaka. Chris, who was once a winemaker in France, wanted a gin to drink neat and tested about 400 recipes before he found the one that he wanted.

The botanicals for Daffy's are carefully sourced to ensure the perfect intensity of flavour and balance for the London Dry-style gin.

Lebanese mint, Balkan juniper, coriander seeds, angelica and orris roots, cassia bark, lemon and orange peels are steeped for four days in wheat grain spirit from France before being slowly distilled for more than nine hours.

The main still is a 700-litre handmade cooper alembic pot still named Robert McGinnis after the artist who painted the artwork for the screen print which is fired on to the glass bottles.

When Chris wrote to the American illustrator, who is famous for his glamorous movie posters, asking him to be involved, his reply was curt: "Dear Chris, please send me your wife."

Daffy's distinctive Goddess of Gin portrait of Mignonne is the result.

In the heart of the Cairngorms National Park, Strathmashie is surrounded by rich foraging land.

Chris runs a distilling school where students forage for ingredients before learning how to create their own gin and then making it – around that famous tasting room table.

SUMMERHALL DISTILLERY

[Pickering's Gin]

Edinburgh
pickeringsgin.com
First gin: March 2014
Tours available

Summerhall is the distillery in the old vet school dog kennels. As claims to fame go it's certainly unusual but it's only one quirky aspect of this gin enterprise.

It is the home of many inventions conjured up by founders Marcus Pickering and Matt Gammell since 2013 when they started transforming the derelict space into a still house.

Not only have they created the popular Pickering's gin brand, but they hit the headlines in style with the launch of the first Christmas gin baubles in 2014.

The distillery is home to two copper stills – Emily and Gertrude – and an innovative bain-marie distilling system created when Matt and Marcus were first developing the distillery.

The long-time friends had been business partners for more than a decade when they were involved in the redevelopment of the site of Edinburgh's Royal Veterinary School – the Dick Vet.

Prompted by a 1947 gin recipe from Bombay sent to Marcus by a family friend and spotting the potential of the kennels, the pair set about building a distillery.

Initially, it was a personal project intended to satisfy their own gin needs but soon it became a commercial enterprise.

Historically the gin drunk in Bombay used local spices and was flavoured to counteract the bitter anti-malarial tonic of the day.

Matt and Marcus adapted the original nine-botanical recipe to suit modern tastes by replacing cinnamon with angelica root and Pickering's Gin was born.

The Bombay recipe was subsequently released as Pickering's Original 1947 Gin. Since then there's been a Navy strength release instigated by the Royal Edinburgh Military Tattoo and in its honour dressed in a bearskin headdress.

It is the Tattoo's tartan which adorns the Scottish Botanicals release which features milk thistle, bog myrtle, Scots pine and heather.

Ever the inventors, Matt and Marcus wondered what would happen if they aged their gin in whisky-soaked casks.

The result is a collection of Oak Aged gins which capture the characteristics of the casks' previous inhabitants.

As for those other quirky inventions, Summerhall is the birthplace of Engine 47 – a former airport fire engine re-engineered to dispense gin cocktails.

TARBRAXUS DISTILLERS

[Pentland Hills Gin]

Tarbrax, West Lothian
www.pentlandhillsgin.com
First gin: November 2018

Gin making was an epiphany in a hot tub for Phil and Tabatha Cox. After 35 years working with the armed forces, Phil decided it was time to work for himself.

And gin would be his thing … so he set about learning the craft – and bought a still (now called Douglas).

Seventeen months later, Pentland Hills Gin was launched. "We live in the middle of nowhere, surrounded by fantastic views.

Living with our sheep, dogs, cats and everything we've tried to do is reflective of the environment we live in," he says.

Up in the Pentland Hills, south-west of Edinburgh, they use their own water, solar panels and the design etched on the bottle is of their dog Panza and the stunning view on their doorstep.

The gin itself owes much to Tabatha's taste and alongside the juniper, coriander, pink pepper pods, orris, angelica and cardamom, there is cocoa, mint and orange.

It has a warmth from the cocoa and cardamom and a floral hint from the mint.

The bottle design is by Lester Darling and, with the environment in mind, the robust packaging they use for posting means that it can be reused to return the bottles to Tarbraxus. "We'd like them to come back so we can fill them again," adds Phil.

TIREE WHISKY COMPANY

[Tyree Gin]

Isle of Tiree
www.tyreegin.com
First gin: July 2017

Hebridean gins often feature special botanicals from their island shores and Tiree's gin continues that tradition.

It uses six botanicals foraged on the island – eyebright, ladies bedstraw, water mint and angelica – and kelp and sea-belt collected from its seas.

Tiree's rich harvest owes much to its position on the Atlantic fringe of the Inner Hebrides.

Only 12 miles long and three miles wide, the flat fertile island has a mild (but windy) climate thanks to the Gulf Stream.

It is on the machair, the rich low-lying land with its sandy soil which makes up a quarter of the island, that many of the botanicals are collected.

The kelp is taken from the large kelp forests in the Atlantic waters offshore. Until the 20th century, this seaweed – used as food, fertiliser and medicine – fuelled a key island industry.

For islanders, Ian Smith and Alain Campbell it was important to capture the flavour of their home when their whisky company launched a gin.

The two musicians had created Tiree Whisky Company to promote the island's whisky heritage: it is said that the island was once home to 50 distillers.

Using the old spelling of the island, Tyree Gin was launched at the 2017 Tiree Music Festival.

Made with the island botanicals at the Thames Distillery in London, the goal was always to distill and bottle the gin on Tiree.

In the autumn of 2018, the distillery started to take shape, with the Genio still arriving in November and production starting in the spring of 2019. The site was previously the base for the building company which Ian's late father ran.

TROSSACHS DISTILLERY

[McQueen Gin]

Callander, Perthshire
mcqueengin.co.uk
First gin: June 2016
Tours available

Dale and Vicky McQueen have been on an adventure in flavour. It started with an ambition to create a more "tasteful" gin – by distillation alone.

With their still, Little Maggie, they raised eyebrows as they created flavours unheard of before.

Sweet Citrus, Spiced Chocolate Orange, Smokey Chilli, Mocha Rich and Chocolate Mint have set the gin world talking – and won numerous fans for the Trossachs Distillery.

Such is the popularity of the McQueens' gins that in the spring of 2019 they expanded their distillery, increasing capacity to more than 2 million bottles a year.

Those unexpected flavours owe much to the chemistry between Dale, a former chartered mechanical engineer and sales professional, and Vicky, an experienced chef with a flair for culinary creativity.

Having made the decision to make gin, but long before they had a distillery, they had bought Little Maggie from southern Germany intent on their quest for tasteful flavours.

To achieve them they use a unique distillation method which sees the botanicals left to macerate in hot spirit overnight.

All the flavours in the gin come from the distillation process.

Having started with four groundbreaking flavours, it was in November 2016 that they launched their Super Premium Dry Gin.

Its Macedonian juniper, grapefruit, lime, vanilla and grains of paradise create a gin with both a creamy rich vanilla sweetness and a crisp lime finish.

Further innovations have followed with one of the most notable being in honour of Dale's love of chilli.

Smokey Chilli Gin has three types of chilli which add smoke and heat to what is still a gin.

VERDANT SPIRIT CO
[Verdant Dry Gin]

Dundee
www.verdantspirits.co.uk
First gin: April 2017

Dundee's history is entwined with the jute industry. Part of its legacy are the large mill buildings where up to 50,000 people across the port city once worked.

The engine house of the Edward Street Mill is now home to the Verdant Spirit Co, founded by Andrew McKenzie.

A passionate foodie, Andrew had been working in the high-octane world of Formula 1 motor racing as the creative head of its marketing arm, before he moved to Dundee in 2000.

The move opened up the chance to pursue his food and drink interests and it was while studying for his MSc in food and drink innovation at Abertay University that the potential of the craft spirits industry caught his attention.

His business – named after one of the Dundee's most familiar jute mills the Verdant Works - grew from there.

The distillery is home to Little Eddie, a 500-litre iStill which can operate as either a column or pot still.

The gin created is inspired by the trading destinations of Dundee's sailors. Its botanicals – juniper, coriander seed, lemon peel, bitter orange, cassia bark, orris root, green cardamom, angelica, liquorice, grains of paradise – come from all over the world.

When Andrew found the engine house, serendipitously it emerged that a previous owner of his own home had been the mill owner John Sharp.

The distillery is being extended to include a visitor centre and some of Sharp's belongings will be used to illustrate the building's heritage.

WEE FARM DISTILLERY

[Drovers Gin]

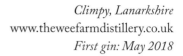

Climpy, Lanarkshire
www.theweefarmdistillery.co.uk
First gin: May 2018

A still on a farm is nothing new – illicit spirits and smuggling are part and parcel of rural Scotland's history – but the gin from this one is inspired by a modern farmer's passion for her livestock.

Jenny and Stephen McKerr had bought a small farm in the hills of Lanarkshire in 2017 and much as they were committed to rearing beef and sheep, they knew needed to bring in additional income.

With a passion for gin, Jenny decided to create one which celebrated Scottish farming and paid respect to the values, traditions and spirits of farmers who put food on our tables every day. In particular she envisaged one that would drink well with a steak.

Drovers Gin is the result and the balance of citrus, thistles, heather, pink peppercorns and allspice is clean and refreshing – and pairs perfectly with beef.

It is made on Morag, Jenny's 30-litre micro still, then bottled and labelled in the distillery.

The Wee Farm Distillery also produces gin liqueurs some musing traditional sweets including sherbet lemon, jelly baby and rhubarb and custard, while others are made with seasonal fruit.

Jenny also took the time to bottle a limited edition of Drovers to support the charity set up by Kelso farmer and former Scotland rugby international Doddie Weir. Doddie's Gin raised £2,500 for My Name'5 Doddie Foundation which supports research into motor neurone disease.

WILD ISLAND DISTILLERY

[Wild Island Botanic, High Croft]

Scalasaig, Colonsay
wildislandgin.com
First gin: December 2016

To thrive on an island takes a special kind of person. A certain resilience for when the ferry doesn't get in and a talent for multitasking wouldn't go amiss.

On Colonsay, Chris Nisbet is that sort of person – he is the air traffic controller, a volunteer fire-fighter, brewer and distiller.

In 2007, he was one of the co-founders of Colonsay Brewery which meant there was draught beer for the 120 islanders who struggled to get supplies from the mainland in the winter months.

When Keith Bonnington with a background in whisky and finance man Allan Erskine became shareholders in 2014, Colonsay Beverages turned its attention to adding premium spirits to its portfolio of craft ales.

First was its signature Wild Island Botanic Gin which uses six botanicals – sea buckthorn, meadowsweet, heather flowers and bog myrtle – picked in the spring and summer on Colonsay. It is made in partnership at Langley Distillery in the West Midlands.

Since 2017, Chris has been distilling on the island – at first developing recipes on a 10-litre test still. Then, in 2018, they took delivery of a 250-litre still and were able to release the first island-made gin, Distiller's Cut.

In the spring of 2019, Wild Island's Sacred Tree Gin was renamed High Croft after the land where its autumn botanicals are gathered.

The recipe uses the same blend of brambles, redcurrants, rosehip, elderberries, rowanberries, crab apple, lemon balm, wild water mint, meadowsweet, sea buckthorn, heather flowers and bog myrtle as Sacred Tree, but it is now distilled on the island.

WILD THYME SPIRITS

[Colonsay Gin]

Upper Kilchattan, Colonsay
www.wildthymespirits.com
First gin: March 2017

Colonsay is home to about 100 people, a wealth of wildlife and stunning ocean views. In 2007, a Dundee-trained architect Fin Geekie and his wife Eileen bought a holiday home on the island.

A decade later the house had been transformed into the HQ for Wild Thyme Spirits – and their permanent home.

And they launched Colonsay Gin – a classic London Dry gin made for them at Strathearn Distillery.

Its botanicals are macerated before being slowly distilled and then left to mellow for more than four days.

Inspired by the Hebridean island's natural beauty and its folklore, Colonsay Gin is presented in bottles with stunning artwork by Caroline Vos.

She has brought to life Alva, the mythical red-haired maiden with supernatural powers who guards the Wild Thyme recipes, for the Colonsay Gin label.

Since Colonsay's launch there have been gin liqueurs added to the range.

The site now also hosts the Gin Lover's Retreat holiday accommodation as well as a small distillery and in 2018 came the first island-distilled gin.

Wild Thyme 909 is a hand numbered edition of Colonsay Gin, limited to 909 bottles.

WILLIAM GRANT & SONS

[Hendrick's Gin]

Girvan, Ayrshire
www.hendricksgin.com
First Gin: 1999

William Grant & Sons is the biggest independent whisky company in Scotland and the owner of one of the most familiar modern gin brands, Hendricks. Owner of Glenfiddich, Balvenie and Drambuie, the company operates four malt distilleries in Scotland plus the grain distillery at Girvan where the Hendrick's Gin Palace is located. In 2018, a £13 million expansion of the palace saw it double capacity and there are now six stills.

The original Bennett copper pot still from 1860 has three exact replicas, while the 1948 Carter Head still has also been copied precisely. The two types of stills are integral to the gin making process which master distiller Lesley Gracie devised when the then company president Charlie Gordon wanted to launch a gin with "more character".

Just 500-litres of Hendrick's are distilled at a time, with the Carter Head still used to gently steam some of the 11 botanicals and the Bennett still to steep others. The two different spirits are then married and infused with Hendrick's trademark Bulgarian Damask rose petals and cucumber.

THE KITH & KIN

Kith (one's friends or acquaintances) and Kin (one's relatives)

The Kith & Kin are the gins and makers who didn't make it to the Distilling Clan. They come from a variety of backgrounds across Scotland – and beyond.

There are Scottish distillers who use distilling equipment belonging to other distillers. These "cuckoos" may be in the process of creating their own distillery.

Bathtub gin doesn't require a still to make it, so these makers are included here. They cold compound botanicals or fruit usually over a number of months to create gins bottled at a minimum of 37.5% ABV (alcohol by volume).

There are also gins created in Scotland but made by someone else in an established distillery. The creators of these gins might be making them for shops, hotels, visitor attractions or events. For others, they are commercial brands. Some of the gins use botanicals handpicked from their home area or they might be inspired by the creator's heritage. These gins are made both in Scotland and elsewhere. They have all been included so that you can make up your own mind.

There are sure to be omissions. Not only are new gins launched with amazing regularity, but some successfully hide their light under the proverbial bushel.

ALEXANDER'S GIN

Stonehaven, Kincardineshire
www.facebook.com/alexandersgin
Launched: December 2018

An encounter with the creator of an orange "gin" in the Caribbean set Fred Stockton thinking about making a "proper" juniper-led gin.

Back in the UK, Fred, a gypsy brewer in his spare time from an oil industry career, started to develop his recipe.

He teamed up with Peter Dignan and Richard Pierce at Lost Loch Distillery and with help from Heriot-Watt University pinned down his flavour profile.

"My idea was that you could drink it neat or with lots of tonic," says Fred, who admits it was a selfish creation of something he and his friends would like.

Using blossom, peel and slices of orange, almond and honey alongside the traditional botanicals of juniper berries, coriander seed, angelica root, liquorice root, pepper and mint, Fred has distilled a gin which drinks both ways.

The luxurious sipping quality comes from the almonds and Deeside honey.

Content to be a cuckoo distiller for now, Fred is excited to see where his gin journey will take him.

ANCIENT MARINER

Helensburgh, Dunbartonshire
hebridean-liqueurs.co.uk
Launched: May 2012

The leaky roof of a West Coast church was the starting point for Ancient Mariner Gin.

To raise funds for repairs to the imposing French Gothic church – St Michael and All Angels in Helensburgh – there was a recitation of *The Rime of the Ancient Mariner* at an event in the church.

It was a stormy night and Samuel Taylor Coleridge's poem of adventure on the ocean struck a chord in a town which has close bonds with the sea.

For Roy Lewis, a lifelong sailor, it started him thinking about the possibility of creating a new brand for his company Hebridean Spirits & Liqueurs.

With an established range of niche liqueurs, Roy went in search of sailors' spirits, rum and gin.

Made in London from 100 per cent British grain, Ancient Mariner Gin comes at 50% ABV in square bottles – perfect for taking on board any ship as they won't topple over.

ARCTURUS GIN

Torridon, Ross and Cromarty
arcturusgin.com
Launched: October 2017

The Torridon resort is in one of the most spectacular locations you can imagine.

At the end of a magnificent sea loch with vistas of dramatic mountains, it is the ideal place to escape with its luxury hotel and 58 acres of parkland.

In creating Arcturus, the Torridon Hotel's owner Dan Rose-Bristow wanted to capture the essence of the estate.

Working with Martin Murray at Dunnet Bay Distillery, the gin was conceived with locally-foraged botanicals.

It uses Scots lovage to encapsulate the land, bilberries and rowanberries for the mountains and kelp for the coast, creating an aromatic crisp clean gin with a dry finish.

Its name also captures its surroundings. Stargazing is a special experience under the dark Highland skies and Arcturus is the name of one of the brightest stars you can see.

Like many stars, it has mythical powers and it is said that female deer can only conceive as Arcturus rises.

With deer a common sight around the estate, it made another good reason to choose the name.

Dan admits building his own distillery is under discussion, but, for now, his efforts are focused on creating a gin garden.

Set in the Victorian kitchen garden, it will be dedicated to growing botanicals for the production of the gin.

BARRA ATLANTIC GIN

Castlebay, Isle of Barra
www.isleofbarradistillers.com
Launched: August 2017

It was a dream for Katie and Michael Morrison to make a life for themselves on their home island of Barra. But, having gone to college in Glasgow, the young couple were embarking on careers there.

To realise that dream, they decided to set up a distillery which, as well as being a family business, would create employment opportunities on the island – and a product worthy of their beautiful home.

Michael, who was designing gift packaging for the whisky industry, set about creating a gin using botanicals collected on Barra.

Among the 17 botanicals, their island hero is carrageen, a reddish-purple seaweed collected from the edge of the Atlantic Ocean after the spring tides.

The botanicals are shipped to London where the floral-herbal gin is distilled for them at Thames Distillery. However this was only the first step in their dream journey.

They have also moved home and set up a shop in Castlebay which employs three people and distributes their island-bottled gin. And a distillery is planned, with the still due on the island in 2019.

BIGGAR GIN

Biggar, Lanarkshire
www.biggargin.com
Launched: April 2018

Some place names bring a smile to your face and Biggar is one of those: the audacity of a small market town that thinks big.

And its gin is born of that big vision: created on a small scale with bags of passion and ambition – from its larger-than-life type face to the punchy gin in the bottle.

Created by brothers Stuart and Euan McVicar, Biggar Gin uses botanicals picked in the area including rowanberries and rosehips.

They blame their mother's amazing rowanberry jelly for their interest in the red berries which grow profusely in the area's woodlands. They add sweetness along with some slightly bitter, astringent tones.

Rosehip meanwhile brings both caramel undertones and a sweet perfume.

For now, Biggar Gin is made at Strathearn Distillery.

However, the brothers are in the process of building their own distillery just outside the town, hoping to have it finished in 2019.

The elegant logo is a nod to the town's greyhound coursing club founded in 1821.

Fifty years later, with numbers down, the remaining members changed it into a drinking club, cashing in the fees for fine wines and spirits.

Stuart and Euan are taking the lead from earlier generations of connoisseurs of fine drinks.

BLACKWOODS
VINTAGE DRY GIN

Distil, London
www.blackwoodsgin.co.uk
Launched: 2005

The bottle makes you think Blackwoods is a Shetland gin. Its 2017 vintage uses meadowsweet, cowslip, wild thyme and eyebright which all grow on the Shetland Isles, however where they are handpicked is not clear.

Each year, the recipe is subtly different depending on the availability of the botanicals, so that the 2012 vintage listed sea pink, marsh marigold and meadowsweet among its botanicals. The year of production is clearly highlighted on the label and there are 40% and 60% editions of the gin.

CADENHEAD'S OLD RAJ

Campbeltown, Argyll
www.cadenhead.scot
Launched: 1972

One of Scotland's oldest gins is also one of its most intriguing. Launched at a time when gin was not the most exciting drink around, Old Raj was created by Cadenhead's, Scotland's oldest independent bottler.

It was launched soon after the company was bought by J&A Mitchell & Co, which owns Springbank and Glengyle whisky distilleries.

The owner Hedley Wright took great personal interest in the product and added the saffron personally as he strived for consistency in flavour and colour. Why they settled on the name or the use of saffron are lost in the mists of time, but it has survived.

The botanicals used in the Old Raj spirit – which is made in England – are juniper, coriander, Seville orange peel, liquorice, angelica root, orris, cinnamon, cassia quills and nutmeg. The saffron is added in Campbeltown – after distillation – and bottled at two strengths. In 2017, a spiced edition of Old Raj was added to the range.

CLACHAIG GIN

Glencoe, Argyll
clachaig.com
Launched: October 2017

The Highlands can be a harsh environment, so places where travellers can take refuge have a special space in the landscape. In the heart of Glencoe, Clachaig Inn has been welcoming guests for more than 300 years.

Today it is a modern 23-bedroom hotel owned by the Daynes family who also have a portfolio of self-catering accommodation in the area.

At the inn's three bars, there is a classic gin – smooth and sweet with a citrus finish, from its key botanicals: orange peel, rose petals and honeyberry.

Clachaig Gin, which also has juniper, coriander, grains of paradise and the roots of angelica, liquorice, orris and calamus, is made for the hotel at Strathearn Distillery.

CRAG & TAIL

Dundee
www.cragandtail.co.uk
Launched: September 2018

There is one thing you can't miss about Dundee and that is the Law – the hill that rises steeply from the Tay, right in the centre of the city.

It is evidence of the Ice Age's moulding of the landscape and, in geological terms, it is a crag and tail – a rocky outcrop with a tapering ridge of glacial deposit to one side.

For the team at Huffman's, the distributor of craft spirits and beers based in Dundee and founded by Gregor Maclean and Ramone Robertson, there was no better name for their own gin. After all, they were looking for a well-rounded spirit with a contemporary slant.

As they had already tasted many gins, they harnessed what they knew they liked and set about adding their own twist.

Crag & Tail – made by Lewis Scothern of Distillutions – uses 12 botanicals including elderflower, orange and lemon, with that twist coming from watermelon. Watch out for more simple, classic gins with a modern slant from the team.

DR OSBOURNE'S
NO 46 AND NO 99

Balquhidder, Perthshire
monachylemhor.net
Launched: June 2018

When you are a chef flavour matters. So when two chefs-turned-hospitality-entrepreneurs, Tom and Lisa Lewis, started making gin inevitably they chose botanicals that went well together.

For Lisa the botanicals were elderflower, lemon balm and rosemary, while Tom went for anise, dill and fennel.

They worked with Hamish Martin at the Old Curiosity Distillery to create their individual Dr Osbourne gins using single plant distillates. The results are Lisa's No 99 and Tom's No 46.

When it came to a name, Osbourne works for them both – it's Tom's middle name and Lisa's doctor as a child was known as "the lovely Doctor Osbourne".

The gin brand adds another string to their bow as they develop their business based around the Monachyle Mhor hotel on the banks of Loch Voil.

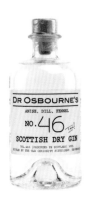
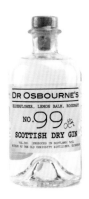

DUNCAN'S GIN

Dunphail, Moray
www.duncansspirits.com
Launched: September 2017

Cuckoo distiller is just the latest entry in Bob and Silvi Duncan's CV. They run Logie Whisky & Wine Shop, but have retired three times already.

They wanted one more adventure when they hit on the idea of distilling gin.

Working with their mentor Walter Micklethwait at Inshriach, they designed a gin which reflected the colours of the Duncan tartan.

The native botanicals – black juniper, green Douglas fir, orange rose hip, white bog myrtle, green sweet cicely, green and purple spear thistle – match up with clear blue spring water for a London Dry-style gin.

DUNDEE GIN COMPANY

Dundee
thedundeegin.com
Launched: December 2016

Peter Menzies is one of Dundee's true characters. He has such wide-ranging interests that many people in the city will know him.

As a Dundonian and the owner of the Vine venue and its mobile catering services, Peter noted the absence of a Dundee gin in his stock.

He decided the gin needed to feature one of the products most closely tied to the city – marmalade.

The Dundee Gin Company's signature Marmalade Gin Liqueur was born and it uses the city's Mackays Dundee Orange Marmalade.

He followed it up with a liqueur featuring another city favourite – Dundee Cake.

Peter has since gone on to have full strength gins created, although he won't disclose where his products are made for him.

The Classic Dry Gin, which uses ten mostly traditional botanicals, lines up alongside Honey & Spice Gin, a sweeter Old Tom-style drink.

ELLIS GIN

Glasgow
www.ellisgin.com
Launched: September 2018

Carol Jackson had been watching the explosion in the craft gin market with interest – she loved sampling the new entrants and observing their growth.

And she spotted a gap in the market – for a premium ready-mixed gin cocktail. Alongside her work in financial services, Carol wrote a business plan and ultimately launched Gin & Mix in February 2017.

These cocktails have no additives or colourings and match her own small batch gin with hand-pressed fruits and roots.

The gin – made for her by Illicit Spirits – has been launched as an independent product – and Carol has quit the corporate life to develop her brands.

"I wanted to produce a coloured flavoured gin – to give me something that was a little bit different to everyone else. So, after much deliberation, we decided on two colours and two flavours," explains Carol.

Ellis Gin No 2 is a red bramble gin which changes to orange when tonic is added. No 3 is a blue butterfly pea gin which turns lilac with tonic.

Carol's imagination doesn't stop there: more variations are planned and the Gin & Mix cocktails are to have a rebrand.

FIDRA GIN

Longniddry, East Lothian
fidragin.com
Launched: September 2018

Fidra is a familiar landmark for those who live near the Firth of Forth. The rocky island off the East Lothian shore is home to puffins, guillemots, razorbills, gulls, seals – and a working Stevenson lighthouse. It was said to be the inspiration for the lighthouse builder's son – Robert Louis Stevenson – when he was writing Treasure Island.

There are also tales of Fidra being used by Dutch gin smugglers as the spot to offload their cargo to Scottish boats.

To Jo Brydie and her friend Emma Bouglet, it seemed the ideal name for the gin they were creating.

With a 5-litre still called Sadie, the friends came up with a recipe that uses juniper, rosehip, elderflower, sea buckthorn, lemon thyme and thyme in a clear London Dry-style gin with a slight salty tang. As they forage on the dunes and shoreline, they often see Fidra. And the slim bottle brings to mind the island's lighthouse.

Fidra Gin is currently made by Inshriach Distillery, but the plan is to make, bottle and label it in East Lothian.

THE GAEL

Dunkeld, Perthshire
thegael.co.uk
Launched: December 2018

One of Scotland's most-played pieces of fiddle music is at the heart of this gin. If you have watched the movie *The Last of the Mohicans* or were at the Edinburgh Military Tattoo in 2000, you will be familiar with The Gael, the piece written by Dougie Maclean.

To celebrate the Perthshire composer's music, The Gael is a single malt gin made at Strathleven Distillery. Five times distilled using malted barley and a blend of traditional botanicals, the inclusion of heather creates a smooth-drinking gin. The bottle has the bonus of including the musical score on the inside back label – if you want to play the tune.

GARDEN SHED GIN

Glasgow
www.thegardensheddrinksco.com
Launched: December 2017

When two Glasgow Warriors rugby players and their wives sat down to dinner one summer evening in 2017, none of them could have imagined it would be the start of a business.

In fact, Ryan Grant who has since retired from professional rugby, Ruaridh Jackson, who plays full back, and their wives, Maxine and Kirstin, came up with the idea for the Garden Shed Drinks Company.

They soon began experimenting to find their ideal gin recipe and develop their branding all within their shared passion for the environment.

They had hoped to create a distillery in a garden shed, but instead distil their gin at Eden Mill, where Ryan had been introduced to the distilling process.

Inspired by the ingredients on their doorstep, Garden Shed Gin is full of florals and spices in a fresh London Dry-style.

The 13 botanicals include juniper, grains of paradise, and some which they literally can find in their gardens – brambles, lavender and dandelion root.

A portion of all profits go to two charities that look after the environment. In an effort to offset their carbon emissions, they plant one tree for every six bottles of gin sold and support the work of the Bumblebee Conservation Trust.

Look out for the quartet's next expression which sees Garden Shed Gin aged in a red wine barrel and taking on some of the wine flavours – and colour - left in the staves.

GIN BOTHY

The fruitful Angus countryside is the source of some of Scotland's most delicious produce. Soft fruit from its fields go to all parts of Britain – and beyond. Berries are delivered fresh or in jams … and now in gin.

Kim Cameron found she had a knack for jam-making and set up the Jam Bothy at her family's farm. When she didn't know what to do with the excess fruit juices, it was her mother who suggested the old country way of soaking them with gin. These fruit-infused gins quickly prompted a name change and the range expanded, using the seasonal produce on her doorstep.

Among the harvest there is rhubarb from the bothy garden, pine needles, heather, sloe berries and gorse flowers from the countryside. Using gin which Kim distils herself at the nearby Ogilvy Spirits, the ingredients are then infused at the bothy in a small-batch process. It takes up to four months and sees the gin turned by hand daily to encourage the intense flavours.

As the range of drinks grow, Kim has expanded her operations. In 2018, she added a Gin Bothy Experience in Glamis to her production bothy, which is in Kirriemuir.

Housed in the former Angus Folk Museum, the new space allows visitors to learn about – and sample – her products. Kim also hopes to have a brewery producing cider and fruit ales on tap during 2019.

GINEROSITY

A gin that supports good causes in its community can only be a tonic for us all. Ginerosity was designed as a social enterprise gin – the first in the world – and its profits have been poured into a range of projects which bring about positive change. At the end of 2018, it announced a partnership with the Grassmarket Community Project in Edinburgh which helps homeless and vulnerable adults. It has also helped young adults from disadvantaged backgrounds gain qualifications, training and work opportunities.

Set up by the founders of Pickering's Gin, Matt Gammell and Marcus Pickering, Dave Mullen of marketing agency Story UK and Chris Thewlis, vice chair of Social Enterprise Scotland, the London Dry gin is made at Summerhall Distillery.

There are ten ethically-sourced botanicals – juniper, coriander, angelica, lemon, lime, orange, lemon myrtle, heather, cardamom and cloves – which give it a crisp modern twist.

GLASSHOUSE GIN

Dornoch, Sutherland
www.carnegieclub.co.uk
Launched: March 2016

The castle once owned by Dunfermline-born industrialist and philanthropist Andrew Carnegie has many riches. Not least the 350 species recorded in a botanical survey of the estate. For Martin Murray of Dunnet Bay Distillery this provided plenty to work with when he was asked to create an exclusive gin for members of the Carnegie Club at Skibo Castle. Having explored the estate, Martin came up with a recipe using bog myrtle, dandelion and the estate's own honey.

Skibo's gardener, Lamont MacCullum and his team picked and dried the plants in a polytunnel before sending them to Caithness for the distilling process. The headline ingredients each bring their own influence, creating a gin which has both a floral sweetness and intense smoothness.

Glasshouse Gin is presented in a striking bottle, with a delicate design incorporating its main botanicals by Pocket Rocket Creative. The name pays tribute to the glasshouses of Skibo which were built by Mackenzie & Moncur, the Scottish firm which designed glasshouses for Kew Gardens and Windsor Castle.

Skibo's glasshouses have been painstakingly restored in recent years and now the vinery, tomato, melon and strawberry houses are bursting with produce for the Carnegie Club's chefs to use.

GLASWEGIN

Glasgow
glaswegin.com
Launched: January 2019

As Scotland's largest city, it didn't go unnoticed that Glasgow didn't have a gin with its name on it. One businessman decided to take matters into his own hands and in 2016 started the process off.

Of course, a Glasgow gin had to be straight to the point with a dry humour and be the epitome of style. The combination of striking branding and a sophisticated gin is the result.

The man with the vision for Glaswegin, Andy McGeoch, has chosen a recipe with eight botanicals which majors on milk thistle, but includes orange flower and chamomile.

Not only does the milk thistle add a smoothness to the gin, it is said to have a restorative effect on the liver.

The stand-out branding is by Paul Gray of Suisse Studio, a design house based in Candleriggs.

Glaswegin is being distilled in the city at Illicit Spirits and there are plans that once it is established it will have a distillery of its own.

GORDON CASTLE GIN

Fochabers, Morayshire
gordoncastlescotland.com
Launched: July 2014

Gordon Castle is a favourite visitor attraction in the north-east of Scotland, offering holiday accommodation, salmon fishing, a café, shop and a delightful walled garden to explore. The castle's popularity owes much to a diversification programme initiated by Angus and Zara Gordon Lennox when they took over running the family estate in 2008.

One of the biggest tasks has been the £1.2 million restoration of the walled garden, which at 8 acres is one of the largest – and oldest – in Britain.

Rare plants, espaliered trees and 350 varieties of fruits, vegetables, flowers and herbs have transformed what was a neglected barren field in 2014 into today's impressive space.

Gordon Castle Gin has been inspired by the garden. Its key botanicals are handpicked within its walls before being sent from Scotland to the distiller who transforms them into the crisp, clean and refreshing gin with subtle notes of lavender and mint.

It is presented in a bottle designed to sit comfortably in Gordon Castle's garden-inspired luxury merchandise.

GRANITE NORTH GIN

Aberdeen
Granitenorthgin.com
Launched: November 2017

Sandy Matheson was climbing Britain's third highest mountain Braeriach in the heart of the Cairngorms when the idea of making his own gin clarified.

The mechanical engineer realised he could capture in a glass the dark forests and pure mountain air of the rugged landscape where he loves to roam.

Ever the perfectionist, Sandy experimented, learning about distilling as he went, before he came up with the combination of botanicals which did the trick.

There's juniper, grand fir needles, grapefruit, lemon and bay leaf in the mix creating a gin which will warm on the coldest nights and refresh on the hottest days.

With his recipe perfected, he went to Persie Distillery where he uses its equipment to distil his gin.

The next step is the construction of his own distillery in the heart of Aberdeen, which is due to open in 2019.

With granite the rock beneath his feat on his Cairngorm adventures, his gin could only be called Granite North. And he presents it in a bottle as solid as any chunk of rock.

HOLYROOD GIN

St Leonard's, Edinburgh
www.holyrooddistillery.co.uk
Launched: August 2018

Holyrood Gin is the trailblazer for a distillery taking shape in the shadow of Arthur's Seat – the hill that dominates the capital's skyline. The distillery is in the 1835-built engine shed of the "Innocent Railway", Edinburgh's first train service.

Founded by Rob and Kelly Carpenter, who set up the Canadian branch of the Scotch Malt Whisky Society, and David Robertson, a former master distiller for the Macallan whisky, the distillery is due to open in 2019.

Whether it is creating single malt or gin, the distillery will focus on putting flavour first in a progressive approach to making spirits.

Until the Holyrood stills are in operation, head distiller Jack Mayo is distilling elsewhere in the city and he used that base to launch four gins during 2018. The Heriot-Watt distilling graduate who had already earned a doctorate in astrophysics, included ten botanicals in both of his first two expressions.

In Holyrood Dry Gin, Jack used traditional botanicals with rosehips and the fresh zest of orange and lemon for a bright clean taste.

Meanwhile, his Pink Gin included fresh raspberries, grapefruit peel and almonds along with the hibiscus and rose petals which give it its colour during a final maceration.

HOUSE OF BOTANICALS
OLD TOM GIN

Aberdeen
www.doctoradams.co.uk
Launched: April 2018

In a lab under the railway arches in Aberdeen, Dr Adam Elmegirab can be found experimenting with flavours. His passion for botanicals has led him over the past decade to create products – in particular bitters – prized by bartenders and drinks enthusiasts.

In 2018, Adam launched his first spirit – an Old Tom gin. A distillation of juniper berries, angelica root, orris root, coriander seed, cassia bark, almond, orange peel and lemon peel is shipped from London to the lab where it is macerated with saffron and chamomile. He quickly followed up with a maple gin based on an old American product made by the Buffalo Distilling Company until 1918.

To his base gin, Adam adds saffron, chamomile flowers and spicy ginger root, before flavouring further and sweetening with maple syrup.

INDIAN SUMMER GIN

Huntly, Aberdeenshire
www.indian-summer.com
Launched: 2014

Duncan Taylor & Company is a name probably best known to those in the whisky industry. The family-owned firm has a bottling plant, a range of blended Scotch whiskies, including Black Bull, and a portfolio of rare casks from "lost" distilleries.

In contrast, its Indian Summer Gin has a more modern feel. Created by the company chairman, Euan Shand, its recipe captures the feeling of a sizzling summer's day by infusing saffron in the UK-made gin. This gives Indian Summer Gin a golden-yellow colour and a warm, rich aromatic flavour.

Its other botanicals include angelica bark, almonds, coriander seed, cassia, juniper berries, lemon peel, liquorice root, saffron, orris root and orange peel. Bottled in Huntly at 46% ABV, it is summer in glass.

ISLE OF ARRAN GIN

Whiting Bay, Isle of Arran
www.isleofarrangin.com
Launched: February 2018

Arran was always referred to as Scotland in miniature – thanks to its hills, lochs and fertile lowlands. Today the island in the Firth of Clyde should be called Scotland's larder: beer, cheese, bread and a host of island-made produce have won foodie fans across the world.

Now, it has its own gin featuring handpicked botanicals – sea lettuce, hogweed seed, meadowsweet, fuchsia, noble fir, angelica and lemon balm – from the island. It is a distinct Dry gin that hints at its seashore and hillside ingredients. It is bold thanks to using double the normal amount of botanicals.

Isle of Arran is the brainchild of four men – Stuart Fraser, George Grassie, George Laird and Ross Hamilton – with a passion for island produce. Stuart owns Bay Kitchen & Stores where the shelves groan with local goodies, while George Grassie is a baker whose bread at Blackwater Bakehouse regularly features foraged ingredients.

They developed the recipe on the island before taking it to Simon Fairclough at Persie Distillery where it is made. With a distillery-visitor experience at Whiting Bay in the pipeline, Stuart and George are busy learning the craft at Persie.

JACK VETTRIANO GIN

Kinglassie, Fife
commercialspirits.com
Launched: June 2018

Jack Vettriano is one of Scotland's most famous modern artists. His vivid paintings are instantly recognisable, capturing an elegance and romance that has won fans around the world.

Stephen Anderson is the founder of Commercial Spirits, a family business which turns concepts into bespoke whisky, rum, vodka, brandy and gin brands. He is based not more than a dozen miles from Vettriano's birthplace, so creating a limited edition gin celebrating the artist's work was a natural fit.

Made at Langley Distillery in Birmingham, the London Dry-style Jack Vettriano Gin uses nine botanicals and is hand bottled in Fife.

These bottles are collectors' items, with four designs, each featuring a different one of Vettriano's classic paintings – The Singing Butler, Billy Boys, Along Came a Spider and A Kind of Loving. Each edition is limited to 2,500 bottles, with 100 of them signed by the artist. However, three of the signed bottles were immediately auctioned to raise funds for the Prince's Trust Scotland.

Keep an eye on Commercial Spirits for more high-profile creations which Stephen is working on.

JAGGI GIN

Dundee
www.jaggigin.com
Launched: September 2016

As the emblem of Scotland, thistles are a familiar sight embellishing Scottish products. Not many can claim to be made from them. Jaggi Gin – named after the Scots word for prickly – uses thistle as one of its key botanicals.

The Jaggi Citrus Gin adds thistle to juniper, coriander, orange bay leaf and nutmeg for a sherbety flavour, tempered by a slight spiciness. Meanwhile the Botanical gin uses berries for a sweetness, while Jaggi Sweet is a mellow almost Old Tom-style gin. All three are made for Jaggi by Strathearn Distillery in Perthshire. As 2019 dawns, Jaggi is being updated so expect to see new branding and expressions on the shelves.

JAMES KEILLER ESTATES' DUNDEE DRY GIN

Dundee
Launched: December 2017

Toast and marmalade go together almost as well as gin and tonic. And it is a Scot who is credited with inventing marmalade as we know it today.

The story goes that a Spanish ship docked in Dundee in the 1760s to shelter from a storm. On board were Seville oranges which were so ripe they would not make it to their intended destination.

James Keiller, who had a grocery shop in the city, saw an opportunity and bought the fruit. His mother Janet created a preserve with the bitter-tasting oranges and, as they say, the rest is history.

Janet's recipe is still the basis for modern marmalades and Keiller's Dundee Marmalade – in its distinctive stone jars – became known all over the world.

With its citrus core, it was only a matter of time before there had to be a marmalade-inspired gin. And there is no better company to have it made than the business which carries the Keiller name.

James Keiller Estates' Dundee Dry Gin was created and distilled by Andrew Mackenzie of the Verdant Spirit Co.

The bottle takes inspiration from the original Keiller marmalade jar and is crafted from white porcelain.

JINDEA GIN

Aberdeen
www.jindeagin.com
Launched: May 2017

The use of tea in gin seems an inevitable step, given that the hot beverage is one of the most popular botanical drinks in the world. This gin uses Darjeeling tea which is noted for its gentle aromatic and floral qualities. The artisan tea gardens at the foot of the Himalayas produce less than 1 per cent of India's total tea production and the spring harvest produces the most prized of these rare black teas.

The first Jindea Single Estate Tea Gin was made using 2016's spring harvest of Goomtee Exotic Thunder Darjeeling tea. The next release –

out in April 2019 – takes early 2017 leaves from the Okayti Organic Tea Estate. These thoughtful gins are the brainchild of three drinks industry professionals – Matthew Dakers, Jack Rackham and Aberdeen-based Adrian Gomes, who owns two bars and the events company 10 Dollar Shake.

Jindea's ten botanicals – the tea along with juniper, lemon, grapefruit, coriander, ginger, fennel, cardamom, cinnamon and angelica – come together in a single pot still distillation in France to a create a bold citrus-forward gin.

Watch out for future releases featuring tea from other parts of the world.

KOKORO GIN

Edinburgh and Nagano, Japan
www.facebook.com/kokorogin
Launched: August 2016

A walk in a Japanese woodland was the start of a journey into gin for Edinburgh entrepreneur, James Nicol. In the Afan Woods in the highlands of central Japan, James was introduced to the sansho berry by his Uncle Nic, a conservationist who had been buying up and restoring neglected woodlands.

Sansho, which has a citrus flavour, a warm pepper finish and a tongue tingling sensation, has been used in Japan to season food for over 3,000 years. As a natural flavour enhancer, it stimulates the taste receptors in the brain, making flavours more intense.

Back in Edinburgh, James set about using it to design a London Dry-style gin with a Japanese heart. Naturally it had to be named after the Japanese word for "heart".

Kokoro's sansho berries – handpicked in Uncle Nic's woods – give a unique heart to the gin's other botanicals – juniper, lemon peel, sweet orange, almond, angelica root, liquorice, savoury and coriander seeds.

LENZIE GIN

Lenzie, Dunbartonshire
www.lenziegin.co.uk
Launched: June 2018

Billington's is a deli in Lenzie, the town which sits about six miles north of the centre of Glasgow. Run by Mark and Sue Billington, the award-winning shop and eatery is a treasure trove of homemade and artisan food and drink. The only thing missing was their own gin.

Mark and Sue took months of research to decide on the recipe for their fresh fruity gin, which is made at Distillutions for them.

Their lead botanicals are bilberry and cranberry which grow on Lenzie Moss, the area of peat bogs and woodland on the edge of the town.

Another six are distilled with the berries before the gin goes into a bottle adorned with a label designed by Sue.

LIND & LIME GIN

Leith, Edinburgh
leithdistillery.com
Launched: November 2018

Leith has played a key part in Scotland's drinks industry over the years. It has had both gin and whisky distilleries, received many bottles of 18th-century Dutch jenever and from the 14th century was an important trading post for barrels of wine, sherry and port.

The empty barrels were then used by merchants to store whisky which in time became the norm for maturing whisky.

As a port, Leith's sailors were at the heart of its success but they travelled in difficult conditions and were often in poor health.

In the Scottish Enlightenment, when great minds came up with ideas that would change the world, Dr James Lind observed that citrus fruits prevented scurvy. From 1867, the law demanded ships carry lime or lemon juice, and it was in Leith that Rose's Lime Juice was born in 1868.

When Ian Stirling and Paddy Fletcher, childhood friends and founders of the Port of Leith Distillery, were looking for a name for their first spirit, the doctor seemed to capture a flavour of the area's heritage. Naturally the gin incorporates lime among its seven botanicals which also include juniper and pink peppercorns to balance the citrus.

The Port of Leith Distillery, which will be Scotland's first ever vertical distillery when it opens beside the Royal Yacht Britannia in 2020, is currently housed at the Tower Street Stillhouse, where Lind & Lime is made.

LOCHABER GIN

Fort William, Inverness-shire
lochaber-gin.com
Launched: September 2017

Lochaber Gin has been created by the team behind Deli Craft and Blas, two businesses at the heart of the Lochaber area, in Fort William. Using botanicals to evoke the area, it is distilled for them at Persie Distillery.

The label features an illustration by Lucy Joy of the hills which give a dramatic backdrop to Fort William.

The Sleeping Lady is familiar to people in the area who know that with the light in a certain way, you can make out a peaceful figure keeping watch over all who pass by.

MACKINTOSH GIN

Dronley, Angus
www.mackintoshgin.com
Launched: October 2018

James and Deborah Mackintosh were big gin fans – and gin festivals were a favourite destination when they moved home to settle in Angus after globetrotting with work. Soon they had amassed an impressive collection of gins and as they bought bottle number 50, they joked they should make their own.

Two years later they had done just that. Now Mackintosh Gin is made for them in small batches at Distillutions in Arbroath.

As they developed the recipe they were keen to showcase the produce of the fertile lands of Angus. When it came to choosing the botanicals for Mackintosh Gin, elderflower was a no-brainer since it grows not two minutes from their home. It was also something they remembered from childhood being made into syrups. They were looking for a fresh London Dry-style gin with floral and citrus flavours and by using real grapefruit among their nine botanicals they have added real depth to the gin's summery citrus notes.

When it came to designing a logo, James and Deborah were keen to continue with the Angus theme and the lovers' knot they use is based on one carved into a 9th-century Pictish stone found near Meigle.

MADDERTY MICRO

[Nudist, Cailleach and Poshist gin]

Crieff, Perthshire
maddertymicro.com
Launched: June 2017

With quirky names, you just know the gins are going to be different. And at Madderty Micro, Russell Wallace has certainly created drinks which grab the attention. It all started as a hobby for Russell who was inspired by the rich sloe gins made by generations of his own family. However, with many fruit gins bottled as liqueurs at 20% ABV, Russell wanted to craft them as full gins at 37.5% ABV. To keep the rich fruit flavours he decided to compound them in small batches by infusing whole, usually fresh, botanicals into a base spirit – without distillation.

He needed a base gin to work with, which is where the Nudist comes in. It is compounded using citrus botanicals and some aromatic dried spices

inspired by a love of Asian cuisine. Raspberries, rhubarb, blueberries are just a few of the Scottish fruits that Russell adds to the Nudist to create his range of flavoured gins.

Ever the experimenter, Russell distilled (using the Strathearn Distillery still) the Nudist's botanicals along with Scots pine needles, chamomile flowers and blackcurrants creating the Poshist Gin.

Another quirky gin is Cailleach, or a witch in Gaelic mythology. In the bottle, Cailleach is blue and shimmers when shaken. A little botanical magic means it turns pink with a mixer.

MCGIN

Glasgow
www.mcgin.co.uk
Launched: May 2018

McGin aims to be a proper Glasgow gin, authentic and unpretentious, with a great sense of humour, like most Glaswegians. And that was the bottom line for Celeste McGinn when she was creating it.

Using her experience of owning pubs in the city for more than 25 years, she wanted a drink that appealed to people from all walks of life and of all ages; a gin that could be drunk in a simple gin and tonic or in a crafty cocktail.

Made at the Glasgow Distillery, it uses eight botanicals – juniper, rosehip, blackberry leaf, angelica root, lemon peel, orange peel, coriander and liquorice – to create this gin of the people.

And the label is a wry take on Glasgow women making their own drink at home – in the bath tub – when they weren't allowed in pubs.

MCLEAN'S GIN

Strathaven, Lanarkshire
www.mcleansgin.co.uk
Launched: September 2017

McLean's Gin hit the headlines in 2017 for coming from the smallest gin lab in Scotland – it was a cupboard in a tenement flat in Glasgow.

Today Colin and Jess McLean have moved production of their range of compound gins to a purpose-built unit in the countryside.

It all started with a gin-making kit which Colin, a mechanical engineer, turned into a Valentine's Day gift for his fiancée Jess, a doctor.

Loving the result, they started making their own gin as Christmas gifts and so what is now McLean's Signature Gin was born.

It has an up-front kick of rich aniseed along with fresh Seville orange, sweet Scottish rose petals and spicy cubeb berries and it's very different from the other gins in the McLean range.

For instance, there's Floral gin which is violet until tonic is added when it turns pink. It combines rose, hibiscus, orange blossom, cardamom and fennel pollen in a fresh gin with a spicy finish.

Then, when they got married in June 2018, Colin and Jess created Something Blue, using their favourite botanicals, tonka bean and bachu leaf.

Originally a limited edition, it is now one of the core range, which also includes the gloriously pink Cherry Bakewell gin.

NERABUS ISLAY GIN

Nerabus, Islay
www.islayginltd.com
Launched: May 2018

Heather is one of the most iconic features of the Scottish landscape. As the summer draws to an end, the moors take on the purple sheen of its flowers.

On the Rhinns – the peninsula to the south-west of Islay – Nerabus Gin was created using some of that heather.

Ian Gow – after a 30-year career in science – put his lab skills to the test in creating a unique Dry gin that would capture the essence of the Hebridean island.

Best known as the home of the smoky whisky, Islay is also a fertile island with a wealth of wildlife including deer and migrating birds and there was plenty of inspiration for Ian and his wife Audrey.

After testing half a dozen recipes using the wild heather which grows on their doorstep, Nerabus gin uses nine core botanicals and island water alongside the August-harvested heather.

Made on the island, Nerabus was launched at the Islay Festival with hog roast and music in Bruichladdich village hall, not far from the hamlet of Nerabus where the Gows live.

NO 25

For more than 150 years there has been a hotel at the east end of Edinburgh's George Street. It has been one of the city's grand gathering places, witness to countless balls, conferences and weddings. By 2017, the George Hotel had undergone extensive renovations and, as part of its relaunch as the Principal Hotel, the general manager Andreas Maszczyk had a gin created.

Principal Gin was destined for the hotel bar, the Printing Press whose entrance is at No 25 George Street. After the sale of the hotel to InterContinental, the gin has changed its name to No 25. It is still the same gin that was developed by Ray Clynick, who was a regular guest at the hotel. The distiller of Oro Gin and co-founder of the Dalton Distillery uses botanicals which reflect the international guests he met at the hotel. Notes of Spanish citrus, French lavender and Italian violets shine in this smooth London Dry-style gin.

ONE SQUARE GIN

A hotel bar is always a cosmopolitan place and One Square at the Sheraton Grand Hotel has a truly international clientele.

As one of the city's best stocked gin bars, it also showcases global flavours, with botanicals from all over the world.

When the opportunity to create an exclusive gin for the bar with an Edinburgh distillery arose, it seemed an ideal mix.

Working with Marcus Pickering and Matt Gammell of Pickering's, One Square Gin was the result. It has 15 botanicals which work together to create a citrusy easy-drinking London Dry gin.

The botanicals come from across the world. Scottish

heather and bog myrtle are found close to home, while the Mediterranean liquorice and orris root which add a heady kick, are from further afield.

And of course, it had to be presented in a distinctive square-shaped bottle.

ORKNEY GIN COMPANY

Isle of Burray, Orkney
www.orkneygincompany.co.uk
Launched: June 2016

Bathtub gin was traditionally a labour of love, made at home with ingredients from the garden or hedgerows and drunk with friends and family.

Modern-day compound gin involves a labour-intensive process which creates gins with distinct intense flavour profiles.

Gary and Andrea Watt had been making their own gin for ten years before they thought about creating a business around it. It took a year for them to put everything in place and come up with the recipes for Johnsmas and Mikkelmas.

Both gins are based on the botanicals growing in Orkney. Johnsmas reflects the refreshing floral notes of midsummer, while Mikkelmas captures the islands' harvest celebrations at the Mikkel feast. They use kegs containing different botanicals which are infused in seven-times distilled neutral grain spirit and go through a six-stage filtering system before being blended in small batches.

Having launched Rhubarb Old Tom in 2017, the team moved in 2018 into new premises which overlook the fourth Churchill Barrier. The barriers were built in 1940 to protect the naval anchorage of Scapa Flow where at the end of the First World War the German Fleet had been scuttled.

Gary and Andrea have created a Navy strength Old Tom style gin called Johannistag (the German for midsummer) to commemorate the centenary of the ships being sunk.

THE ORRY

Eaglesham, Renfrewshire
www.facebook.com/TheOrryGin
Launched: June 2018

People make gins for a surprising number of different reasons but creating one for a beer festival is one of the less expected.

Eaglesham, the village on the southern edge of Glasgow, has had a beer festival since 2015 and each year it has grown in popularity. The festival organiser Fraser Wilson worked with Colin McLean of McLean Gin to create a compound gin for the event.

The smoked black cardamom and honey blossom flavoured gin was such a hit that it has since found a more permanent home as Eaglesham's own gin. Its name refers to the Orry – 15 acres of common ground in the centre of the village.

PARTRIDGES
CHELSEA FLOWER GIN

London
www.partridges.co.uk
First gin: May 2017

Celebration is at the heart of Partridges Chelsea Flower Gin. The family-run royal grocer in London created the gin in collaboration with Martin Murray of Dunnet Bay Distillery to mark its 45th anniversary and to co-incide with the annual RHS Chelsea Flower Show, which takes place near its main store.

The London Dry gin created by Martin in the distillery close to the home of the great, great, great grandmother of the store's owners, the Shepherds, has a light sweetness and gentle notes of spice.

It has 19 botanicals including rose petals, marigold, verbena, cassia bark and juniper, with the subtle rose flavour commemorating the historic links of flower nurseries with Chelsea, where the Partridges business started.

A second – bergamot infused – edition of Chelsea Flower Gin was created to celebrate the royal wedding of Prince Harry and Meghan Markle in 2018. The gins are exclusively available in Partridges' two London stores.

PERTH GIN

Perth
www.perthgin.com
Launched: March 2018

Distilling has very deep roots in Perthshire. There were 44 distilleries in the county 200 years ago and in the last century some of the most famous whisky brands – Bells, Dewars and Famous Grouse among them – were based in Perth.

By the dawn of the 21st century, distilling had disappeared from the city, so in 2016, when Iain McDonald and Elaine Brady founded Perth Gin, it was an opportunity to create a product which chimed with the city's heritage. Iain, who remembers playing near the bonded warehouses, was determined to create a distillery in the city centre and that dream will become a reality in 2019.

Until it is up and running, Iain, Elaine and head distiller Gerard Macluskey – who brings experience from Tanqueray and several craft gins – have been distilling at Strathearn Distillery.

Their gin is a classic juniper-led London Dry-style with coriander, spicy and savoury notes and a hint of citrus. Its blend of 15 botanicals is distilled in small batches on 100-litre Hoga stills.

The distilling environment will be replicated in the Perth Distillery when it opens in sight of the iconic Tay bridge built in 1771 by John Smeaton. That is the bridge which features on the bottle label.

PILGRIM'S

St Andrews, Fife
www.pilgrimsgin.com
Launched: April 2018

That St Andrews was once an important religious centre is apparent by the remains of the cathedral which dominate the town. Pilgrims journeyed there through the Middle Ages, sustained on their walk by food from the wayside communities – and water from natural springs. The spring on the Balmungo Estate, just south of St Andrews, would have been used by the weary pilgrims as they finally had their destination in sight.

Today, its waters are being used by Allan Drysdale to create Pilgrim's. Juniper, together with coriander, angelica, grapefruit and liquorice root give the gin both savoury and fresh notes which are rounded out by blackcurrants.

For now, Allan is using the cold compound process to create his gins but he hopes to set up a distillery in 2019.

In the meantime, he's created a range of gin liqueurs pairing a soft fruit with a herb or spice to compliment his original gin.

PRINCE OF ORKNEY GIN

Roslin, Midlothian
www.rosslynchapel.com
Launched: September 2017

Rosslyn Chapel is arguably one of Scotland's most famous religious buildings. And that is thanks to the American author Dan Brown featuring it in his book *The Da Vinci Code* and the film-makers then using it as a location for the movie starring Tom Hanks.

In the book's wake, visitor numbers increased at the 15th-century gothic chapel to the south of Edinburgh and a visitor centre was opened in 2012.

What is probably less well known is the chapel's links with Orkney. It was founded in 1446 by Sir William St Clair, the third Prince of Orkney.

To celebrate these links, the chapel trust worked in partnership with Orkney Distilling on a gin which includes a number of Orkney-grown botanicals.

It is on sale in the shop, where its income supports the conservation of the chapel.

RAVEN GIN

Inverurie, Aberdeenshire
www.ravengin.com
Launched: May 2018

The powerful aromas which filled the air as gin was emptied from the still entranced the two brothers and left them pondering the possibilities of the craft. This encounter with the Botanist's still on Islay set Peter and Callum Sim on the road to creating Raven Gin. Back home in Aberdeenshire, the siblings worked with Mike Bain at Deeside Distillery to experiment and perfect a recipe.

Raven Gin is unusual in using mandarin as a botanical in a long slow distillation. It is then rested and married for about a month before bottling.

This results in a smooth Dry gin with the modern slant of mandarin against its six traditional botanicals.

When they wanted a name, the brothers turned to Callum's long-held interest in Norse mythology. Two ravens – Huginn and Muninn, meaning thought and memory – serve Odin, the king of the gods. And Hrafn means raven in old Norse. Callum and Peter named their first release Thought & Memory, using Hrafn for their first limited edition - a winter gin using frankincense and myrrh.

REDCASTLE GIN

Carmyllie, Angus
redcastlegin.co.uk
Launched: July 2017

Whether you think of it in terms of beer, horses or gin, Redcastle itself is a ruined fortified tower house which sits dramatically above Lunan Bay on the Angus coast. Built to keep out the Vikings, the castle lands have been in John Anderson's family for many years and the last Baron of Redcastle was his Uncle Jack. The horses are Clydesdales which John has bred for more than three decades and the beer comes from his Redcastle Brewery.

John teamed up with Fiona Walsh, a drinks industry consultant, to launch Redcastle Gin. It is based on the family bon viveur Uncle Jack, with botanicals which capture his spicy personality and zest for life.

Among the blend of 13, are kaffir lime leaf – to enhance other citrus flavours – and pink peppercorn to reflect his personality.

The recipe was created by Fiona with the help of Lewis Scothern at Distillutions where it is made, with the bottles filled, sealed and labelled by hand at the brewery. However, distilling will move in house at the brewery in 2019. And Fiona and John have gone on to add gin liqueurs and a spiced rum to the Redcastle stable.

THE ROYAL YACHT BRITANNIA GIN

Leith, Edinburgh
www.royalyachtbritannia.co.uk
Launched: June 2016

Even the most Scottish of gins can include botanicals from far-flung parts of the world.

In the past, ships from Scotland would have sailed to the places they grow. One ship that has probably visited more ports than most is the Royal Yacht Britannia.

As the Queen's floating palace, Britannia travelled more than 1 million nautical miles, calling at 600 ports in 135 countries between 1953 and 1997.

The style and attention to detail maintained for the Royal Family as they made their official voyages are legendary.

Britannia's state functions had the same formality and grandeur as any of the royal palaces and a roll-call of famous names were entertained.

The Royal Family spent many days aboard and to mark the Queen's 90th birthday, a gin was created at Summerhall Distillery not far from Leith, where Britannia is now moored.

Britannia Gin uses 16 botanicals, each originating from a port the yacht had visited.

SMITHIES GIN

Arbroath, Angus
smithiesgin.com
Launched: August 2018

When you own a shop which stocks more than 200 gins, you build up a lot of knowledge about the spirit.

No surprise then that Patti Smith who has one such shop – Smithies Deli in Arbroath – decided to create her own gin. With her two daughters Jill and Beth, the trio were inspired by their garden. It had belonged to Patti's father and they all have happy memories of him tending the hundreds of different fruits, flowers and herbs.

Distilled for the family in Scotland, Smithies Gin has 12 botanicals including fruits typically found in Angus gardens like redcurrants and gooseberries.

Patti is keen not to dictate how other people drink the smooth gin which has a sharp sweetness from the berries. "We want people to drink it the way they want to drink it," she says.

SQUARE PEG GINS

Vale of Leven, Dunbartonshire
www.squarepegspirits.com
Launched: June 2018

In 2018, five guys from different backgrounds in the drinks industry set about challenging the status quo by creating unique spirits.

Unconventionally Square Peg Spirits' first gin was launched at a festival at Aldi, the discount supermarket chain.

The nationwide exposure for Square Peg Pink Gin meant it was a shrewd start.

The gin is infused with raspberries and blackberries from Perthshire and distilled using Scottish grain at Strathleven Distillery.

There are no artificial colours or sweeteners, just the juniper, coriander seed, lemon peel, and berries giving a fresh fruity blast to the juniper notes.

The five – Andrew Shand, Brian O'Shea, Ricky Christie, Sam Peacock and Simon Ross – quickly followed up with Square Peg Craft Gin, a London Dry-style, citrus-lead gin with a slight spice finish.

Watch out for other spirits from the innovative quintet in the future.

ST ANDREWS GIN CO

St Andrews, Fife
www.standrewsbrewingcompany.com
Launched: November 2017

The St Andrews Brewing Co has been making beers since 2012 – first in a garage and now in a brewery near the town's Botanic Garden.

As the brewery founders say, having made beer for a while you start to think, "Hey, let's make some gin," and so they launched three.

One – Orange, Cardamom and Tonka Bean Gin – is inspired by a sauce once served with scallops at the town's Seafood Restaurant.

The Lemongrass and Ginger Gin has an Asian complexity, with spicy notes from fresh ginger, allspice and kaffir lime leaves.

The Pink Grapefruit Gin is a relatively straightforward refreshing mix of citrus flavours.

The gins are made for the company at Strathearn Distillery.

SUTORS GIN

Tain, Ross and Cromarty
sutorsgin.com
Launched: March 2019

Guarding the entrance to the Cromarty Firth are the Sutors. On the headland to the north is a distillery growing from this rich landscape.

The brainchild of IT specialist Stuart Wells and agronomist Ed Scaman, the distillery will take barley and wheat grown on its doorstep, malt it and make its spirit from scratch. Only a handful of Scottish gin makers do this, and the conversion of a milking parlour into a fully equipped distillery in 2019 has been crowdfunded and taken more than a year.

To the bespoke Sutors spirit, hand-foraged botanicals are added. The hills and shores around the distillery yield watermint, bog myrtle and sea buckthorn for their gin, which is diluted with pure water drawn from deep within the North Sutor.

For Stuart, who as a child helped his grandfather make liqueurs for Christmas, and Ed, who also started young making gins from the sloes, damsons and brambles in his native Lincolnshire, Sutors marks a shared vision of a gin of the land.

In addition to making their own grain-to-glass gin, Ed and Stuart will offer a bespoke gin-making service for the farmers who grow malting barley.

THE TEASMITH

Udny, Aberdeenshire
teasmithgin.com
Launched: December 2016

The pioneers of using tea as a botanical in Scotland are Nick and Emma Smally.

They were inspired by the thriving Victorian tea trade of the North-east of Scotland and in particular by James Taylor from Auchenblae in the Mearns who planted the first tea plantation in Ceylon, now Sri Lanka.

Like many Scots who travelled the world at that time, Taylor is held in high esteem for the way he transformed the island.

The Teasmith gin uses handpicked and hand-rolled black tea from the Amba Estate in Sri Lanka.

The rare tea, which was chosen with advice from the tea consultant Beverly-Claire Wainwright, grows at an altitude of more than 1,000 metres in a small valley above the Ravana Ella Waterfalls.

By choosing only the finest leaves and buds and distilling it on its own, it adds rich aromatic flavours to the gin.

Made at Strathearn Distillery, juniper, coriander, liquorice root, orange peel, rose petals, honeyberry, grains of paradise, orris and calamus root are distilled not once, but twice in traditional copper alembic stills.

The distillates are then carefully blended together, creating a light crisp gin which doesn't actually taste like tea.

TENACIOUS

Dufftown, Moray
www.whiskyshopdufftown.com
Launched: November 2016

To run a small business needs tenacity – even if it is a whisky shop in the heart of Speyside's distillery country. After a successful decade in business, Mike Lord, owner of the Whisky Shop Dufftown was in the mood for celebrating and came up with the idea of creating a gin. Tenacious was the result.

This juniper-led gin, with its notes of citrus and sweet gentle spices, uses ten botanicals. Distilled in Shetland, alongside juniper it combines coriander seeds, angelica root, lemon peel, orris root powder, nutmeg, burdock root, bitter almonds, pink pepper and Szechuan pepper.

Inspired originally by a make-your-own experience at Edinburgh Gin, Mike's recipe was developed for a couple of years before he teamed up with Saxa Vord Distillery to bring his vision to reality for the shop's anniversary. Ever the entrepreneur, Mike, who left a London career in financial services to follow his dream of owning an independent whisky shop, has extended his store's reputation to become a respected gin stockist.

TRUE ORIGINS

Banchory, Aberdeenshire
trueorigins-ginfestival.com
Launched: January 2019

Among the many gin festivals that have appeared in the calendar, True OriGINs is billed as a celebration of Scottish gin. Created by Guy and Mungo Finlayson, True OriGINs lives up to its name and they are adamant that its participants will only be gins "distilled/rectified and bottled in Scotland".

For the brothers, provenance is everything and so when they decided they wanted their own festival gin, they focussed on what went into it and how it was made. Working with Peter Dignan and Richard Pierce at Lost Loch Distillery, Guy created the recipe around what grew in Aberdeenshire.

The first small-batch was Autumn Gin which uses apples, rosehip and heather flowers among a total of ten botanicals.

WHITETAIL GIN

Tiroran, Isle of Mull
whitetailgin.com
Launched: August 2017

On the shores of Mull is Tiroran, a stunning estate with an abundance of wildlife and dramatic countryside.

Close by, nest white-tailed eagles, the UK's largest birds of prey, with a wingspan of more than 2 metres.

These majestic birds were the perfect inspiration when the owners wanted to create a gin for the family estate.

As the marketing says, "Just like its namesake, Whitetail Gin is superior in strength and power. It's also subtle and smooth – as gentle on the palate as a feather drifting down from the sky".

Using botanicals from the island and water from Tiroran's private spring, Whitetail Gin is currently distilled by Charles Maxwell of Thames Distillers in London.

The Mull botanicals he uses include sustainably-harvested sea kelp from nearby Loch Scridain, hand-foraged heather and savoury from the estate and pine from the forest where the eagles nest.

In future, the estate will have its own distillery, which will sit beside the Whitetail coffee shop – and Mull will have its own gin.

TONIC WATER

Few of us can resist a G&T – if it's not the epitome of a summer Saturday, I don't know what is. But things have changed: gone is the obligatory G& "Schhh, you know who" – today it's all about complementing the flavours of each gin's botanicals. On the tails of Scotland's boom in craft distilling, we are seeing the seeds of tonic-making take root.

Admittedly the biggest independent names are Fentimans of Northumberland, Fever Tree of Somerset and Franklin & Sons of London, but Scots are making a stand. Here, we look at four tonic waters from Scotland.

BON ACCORD

Bon Accord Soft Drinks, Edinburgh,
www.bonaccordsoftdrinks.com

Created to complement the flavours of gin by Karen Knowles and her business partner, Nathan Burrough, Bon Accord Scottish Tonic Water uses a little less quinine than other brands. Available in original and light, it has a clean crisp flavour, with a hint of citrus and vanilla. It marks the revival of one of north-east Scotland's most familiar names, for Karen is the great, great granddaughter of the founder of Bon Accord which delivered soda and pop to homes in the area for almost a century from 1903. Today, all the Bon Accord soft drinks are sweetened 100 per cent naturally. *Launched: 2016*

CUSHIEDOOS

Drink Better Ltd, Edinburgh, cushiedoos.com

Unlike a traditional tonic, Cushiedoos has no quinine. Created by former marketeer Andrew Ligertwood, it uses heather, silver birch, yellow gentian, wormwood (artemisia absinthium) and British sugar beet, with water from ancient artesian springs high in the Cairngorms, which is low in mineral content. The heather and birch are wild foraged in the Highlands while the yellow gentian and wormwood are now being grown at the Secret Herb Garden in Edinburgh with a first harvest due soon. Packaged in a smart but witty livery, Cushiedoos has 24 per cent less sugar than many familiar brands. The Cushiedoos name originates from the Scottish word for wood pigeons, who just like the faithful G&T partnership, mate for life. *Launched: 2018*

JUST THE TONIC

Just the Tonic, Glasgow, www.facebook.com/justtonicnobull

This tonic is all about style – no gimmicks: just the aim to create a "great tasting tonic water that is clean and crisp, allowing the gin to sing". It is actually the creation of Hannah Fisher and Craig Strachan, two entrepreneurs based on the Clyde who also run the Start-up Drinks Lab, a contract bottler for small soft drinks companies, and Foal Drinks, a range of craft sodas, sweetened only from natural sources. With that pedigree, the pair were determined to cut to the chase: "Distillers put much thought and attention into creating their individual gins, therefore we wanted to create a tonic water that would allow each of their idiosyncratic styles to shine through and not mask it with too much fuss," explains Hannah. *Launched: 2018*

WALTER GREGOR'S

Summerhouse Drinks, Aberdeenshire, www.waltergregors.com

This was the first of Scotland's tonic waters and it's made just from natural ingredients. Not surprising then that the name was inspired by a respected 19th-century plant expert, the Rev Walter Gregor, and that many of the botanicals it uses are grown in the walled garden he tended in Aberdeenshire. "Our tonics are truly hand-crafted. We grow the botanicals in his walled garden and bottle the drinks in a converted steading a few fields away," explains Claire Rennie, who founded Summerhouse Drinks after a crowdfunding campaign in 2014. The tonic range was expanded to include new flavours – Scottish Raspberry, Spiced, Cucumber & Mint, and Apple & Cinnamon – in 2018. *Launched: 2015*

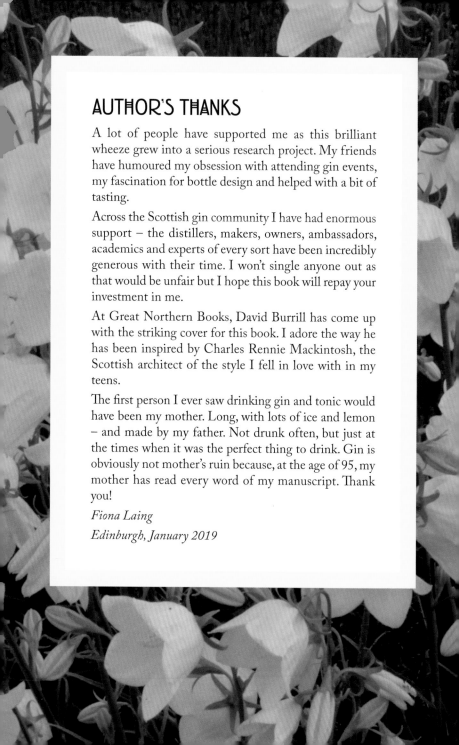

AUTHOR'S THANKS

A lot of people have supported me as this brilliant wheeze grew into a serious research project. My friends have humoured my obsession with attending gin events, my fascination for bottle design and helped with a bit of tasting.

Across the Scottish gin community I have had enormous support – the distillers, makers, owners, ambassadors, academics and experts of every sort have been incredibly generous with their time. I won't single anyone out as that would be unfair but I hope this book will repay your investment in me.

At Great Northern Books, David Burrill has come up with the striking cover for this book. I adore the way he has been inspired by Charles Rennie Mackintosh, the Scottish architect of the style I fell in love with in my teens.

The first person I ever saw drinking gin and tonic would have been my mother. Long, with lots of ice and lemon – and made by my father. Not drunk often, but just at the times when it was the perfect thing to drink. Gin is obviously not mother's ruin because, at the age of 95, my mother has read every word of my manuscript. Thank you!

Fiona Laing
Edinburgh, January 2019

INDEX

Gins, makers and distilleries in the Clan and Kith & Kin listings